ADVANCE PRAISE

"*The Power of Conscious Connection* is a profound and inspiring work that serves as a powerful call to action for leaders and connects our power to drive change. Talia Fox offers practical strategies for operationalizing joy and cultivating a more connected, compassionate culture."

—TEEDRA BERNARD, Chief Talent & Diversity Officer,
TransUnion

"In a world that feels more frantic and divided than ever, Talia illustrates how conscious connection can help us each live our best lives and have the greatest positive impact on those around us."

—DANIEL FEUSER, former CEO

"In an increasingly polarized and deeply complex world, Talia Fox teaches us the simple, everyday habits that each of us can develop to create the deep, lasting, and conscious connections which, in the end, are the very marrow of life."

—LAURA GASSNER OTTING, *Wall Street Journal*
bestselling author of *Wonderhell*

"*The Power of Conscious Connection* is a collection of lessons and habits that Talia provides her audiences to align with the principles to Listen, Observe, Value, and Engage (LOVE), from which our inner power emulates. I am now learning to be a better human by practicing LOVE, a quest that should never end. This requires breaking free of the day-to-day noise and exercising deep cognitive thought to the world around us. I hope the readers will bless our planet through the eyes of LOVE."

—HARVEY JOHNSON, Deputy Assistant Secretary,
Department of Veterans Affairs

"Talia helps the reader with self-discovery and provides a bridge to positive actions. She 'pulls back the curtain' of our experiences and allows us to be directors in our 'own' world."

—SANDRA EDMONDS CREWE, PhD, MSW, ACSW, Dean and Professor of Social Work, Howard University

"*The Power of Conscious Connection* is a profound and practical blueprint for executives and senior leaders. Learning to listen, observe, value, and engage requires continuous development and evaluation."

—COL (RET) DAVID L. MUSGRAVE, Senior Executive Service, Department of Defense

THE POWER OF
CONSCIOUS CONNECTION

4 HABITS TO TRANSFORM HOW YOU LIVE AND LEAD

THE POWER OF
CONSCIOUS CONNECTION

TALIA FOX

Founder and CEO of KUSI Global, Inc.

IDEAPRESS
PUBLISHING

WASHINGTON, DC

IDEAPRESS
PUBLISHING

Ideapress Publishing | www.ideapresspublishing.com

All trademarks are the property of their respective companies.

Cover Design: Faceout Studio
Interior Design: Jessica Angerstein

Cataloging-in-Publication Data is on file with the Library of Congress.

Hardcover ISBN: 978-1-64687-135-3

Special Sales
Ideapress books are available at a special discount for bulk purchases for sales promotions and premiums, or for use in corporate training programs. Special editions, including personalized covers, custom forewords, corporate imprints, and bonus content, are also available.

1 2 3 4 5 6 7 8 9 10

CONTENTS

———

ACKNOWLEDGMENTS

———

To all the remarkable people, businesses, and institutions that I've had the privilege of working with—thank you.

This book is dedicated to you.

Your willingness to take risks, share your stories, and develop conscious leadership practices has been a source of inspiration. I am grateful for the connections we've made and the trust you've placed in me.

Together, we have uplifted each other to new heights, instilling the values of conscious leadership, compassion, and genuine human connection into business and life.

To my dear sons, Elijah and Jaden, your unwavering love and presence in my life have been my greatest gift and leadership opportunity. You have taught me the true essence of love and remind me to stay connected to what matters in this world.

FOREWORD

———

In the pursuit of leadership, one encounters many different styles, theories, and practices. Some are traditional, rooted in the historical context of command and control. Others are innovative, breaking boundaries and pushing the limits of what we know about leading others. And then there is the approach Talia Fox invites us into in her wonderful and valuable book, *The Power of Conscious Connection*.

With wisdom and a deep sense of humanity, Talia shares that leadership is not about a title or position but more about a conscious act of connection. And walks the reader (yes that's you my friend) into a clear understanding of her LOVE system—Listen, Observe, Value, Engage—a powerful framework that roots leadership in the practice of conscious connection, empathy, and mutual respect.

Through her own experience as a leader, alongside decades of professional practice, Talia gives us an unfiltered view into the challenges, triumphs, and transformative power of leading with conscious connection. Her stories are not just inspiring; they are a call to action for every leader to engage deeply, to lead with purpose, and to value the power of connection.

Talia Fox has written a book that is not just powerful; it's absolutely necessary. In a world that is increasingly disconnected, her call for conscious connection is the wake-up call we need to hear. It's a call to action, a call to change, and finally, a call to lead with habits that restore presence and love.

Our world needs more real leaders. Why wait for more of them when you have it in you to become one of them?

—Robin Sharma, #1 worldwide bestselling author of
The Leader Who Had No Title and *The 5AM Club*

PREFACE

———

Through this book, my goal is to light a path of self-discovery and to create a strong bond with you, my reader. To do so, I open my life to you and share experiences that include lessons learned from over 20 years of developing leaders. It is a pleasure to meet you.

This book is the doorway to our very first conscious connection. I hope that our time together will be filled with insights and revelations that can be used to transform any aspect of your life!

My intention is to remind you of your immeasurable worth and inspire you to act. I know that you have the power to shape not just your life but also the course of humanity through the choices that you make. Together, we can find the strength to lead.

For those who are busy, overwhelmed, disengaged, or just exhausted by all the issues in the world, I offer you a simple path and something to focus on. You will not need a big budget, a huge team, or a bookshelf of resources. You will only need patience, commitment, and a little bit of time to reflect on who you are and how you want to spend your time on this earth.

I began writing this book with a goal of elevating others. Back in 2019, when *Conscious Connections* was just a working title, I hoped to uplift changemakers. Not only did I want to empower those with the title and influence to make change *now*, but I also wanted to inspire people who hadn't realized that they, too, have the power to drive change.

Before the book was finished, COVID-19 struck, and the whole world changed. The pandemic isolated us from friends, family, and our whole communities, while nations struggled to combat a deadly new disease and workers struggled to feed their families. COVID-19, combined with a wave of social and political challenges, served as a reminder that we humans want the same things: approval, control, security, connection, and the sense that we are appreciated and valued for our uniqueness.

Crisis often brings us back to an enduring truth—we are all connected. Disconnection is not an option. We are either aware of how our thoughts, feelings, and actions impact the world, or we impact it by accident. The former is a conscious connection; the latter is an unconscious connection. Conscious connections represent both making connections between our behaviors and outcomes and nurturing our connection to each other.

The Power of Conscious Connection details the habits and skills necessary to reconnect to the inner knowing of what we all need to thrive. This knowledge comes at a price—we must be strategic and honest. We must step up to lead as we navigate complex issues such as inequity, bias, exclusion, and disregard for others' identities.

These are all symptoms of a polarized world. The solution is both existential and practical. The truth about the human experience is that we are always shaping a shared destiny. Our decisions impact each other.

What you do, based on the conclusions you come to about the world, will always have a ripple effect on humanity.

I challenge you to seek out the significance in your life, dare yourself to make courageous decisions, cherish who you are, and embrace others with love.

INTRODUCTION

———

My First Conscious Connection: A Colicky Lesson on Going Pro

My son's little body was warm against my chest, his breathing finally slow, and his chin back in a posture of total relaxation. As I rocked him back to sleep, his weight felt comforting, even in my exhausted arms. We were so close; it was like we were one being, rocking together in that dark, silent room.

And, yet, I felt so alone.

I sat in that rocking chair in October 2000 staring down a choice.

I'd given birth to a beautiful, very colicky baby boy, Elijah. With moods ranging from upset to inconsolable, he cried and fussed until we were both beyond exhausted. I was a single mom embarking on a journey that would prove much harder than I'd thought.

As I looked down at his tiny face, I knew I'd barely begun.

I already felt defeated.

Between school, work, and caring for my son, I was losing the battle and the war.

The worst part was my total lack of purpose—at one point, I felt like I knew exactly what I wanted from this life. It felt simple. As a kid, I was full of enthusiasm. I was a chubby eight-year-old who tossed her long braids over her shoulder, put her hands on her hips, planted her feet, and stood strong on her legs—bedecked in Punky Brewster leg warmers—and declared, "That's it! I'm having fun!"

Now, it seemed I was always tired and had a bad attitude. In my utter exhaustion, I felt agitated at everyone and everything. Even my precious baby rarely made me smile. Then, I received the gift of defeat. It was a record-breaking cold winter. The elevator and the electricity in my apartment building were out of commission. I got home after school and work holding my baby in one hand, groceries, a book bag, and a gallon of water in the other. I had to take the stairs to my fifth-floor apartment. I was tired. I was cold. I was done. I ended up crying in the stairwell until the tears just stopped. I felt a calm come over me and was distracted by the faint and peaceful smile on my son's face. It was at that moment that I declared: Something has to change.

I started with one small shift: Each day, I woke up as if my life were a show. I jumped out of bed, stretched my hands in the air, and screamed, "It's game time! I'm a pro!" Although startled at first, the baby eventually started to giggle at my little routine—and the sound of a happy baby is always a game changer.

Then, I worked on my attitude and my perspective. Even when I felt a little irritated, I smiled and decided to choose a different way of existing in the world. I breathed more deeply. I was getting more sleep, and my mother would surprise me with visits (and free babysitting!). And as my mood improved, I started to generate ideas. *Maybe I could start a business,* I thought. *Maybe I could make a difference in someone's life.*

Maybe I could change the world.

That small shift—jumping out of bed and making a daily commitment to showing up—might not seem like much. But I've seen it change lives.

Most people go through their entire lives following the path of least resistance. Locked in a perpetual cycle, they go to work, exist, and keep their heads down, fully expecting the world to bend to their own personal quirks and preferences.

They don't jump out of bed with the intention of improving how they show up for the world. They do not practice living a rich life. Completely absorbed by their problems, some don't jump out of bed at all—they drag themselves through life feeling sad, tired, broken, and disappointed.

I could have easily stayed stuck in that place, watching miserably as my life ticked by. Instead, I recommitted to "going pro" every single day. Years later, I turned my journey of "going pro" into a signature leadership model emphasizing that the foundation of effective leadership is showing up and asking, What does this situation need from me today to be most successful?

> I was conscious of how my choices impacted my outcomes and connected to my power to change them.

I was able to tap into a new level of potential and power that I had never experienced before. It felt like I was unlocking secrets of my own inner strength and purpose. It became clear to me that no matter how challenging the circumstances were, I could determine the course for my life by making intentional choices about what I focused on and how I responded. By connecting with this newfound awareness, it felt like anything was possible. I was conscious of how my choices impacted my outcomes and connected to my power to change them. My journey of self-discovery had begun!

Eight years later, after thousands of hours of studying psychology and leadership, my life changed dramatically. As my knowledge deepened, I came back to that simple shift that turned everything around. I finished college and graduate school and studied strategies to measure and teach concepts like hope and a sense of purpose. I became obsessed with human and social behavior and how our identities shape our choices and our lives. I observed, in detail, how leaders and people from all walks of life interacted and communicated with each other. I became so great at this observation that I could begin to accurately guess the kind of life others lived. Did they have flourishing relationships? Were they financially secure? What kind of leader, boss, or employee were they? It seemed eerily easy to predict outcomes based on how present and connected they were with others. I held some remarkable jobs, eventually establishing my first consulting company. I learned a lot about success and began to define it for myself. I did not define success by money or title, but by how I impacted others.

Have you ever met a person and been inspired by how they live and approach life? Have you ever been with someone who made you feel fearless and worthy of big dreams? If you have not, I will show you how to increase your chances of not only becoming that person, but also of creating armies of those people all around you. I also learned that successful people are making very different choices. They are doing things that are nontraditional and sometimes a bit strange.

As I reflect on my journey, I am struck by how the seemingly small choices I made had the biggest impact on my mental well-being. Sometimes, veering off the well-trodden path of others and choosing a different path can lead to life-altering decisions.

As a single mother, I was warned against pursuing entrepreneurship, but it felt like the right choice for me. It was risky, for sure, but I was drawn to the idea of creating something meaningful and having the freedom to apply my talents on my own terms. Yet, still, it was an uncertain path.

But it wasn't just the decision to start a business that took me off the beaten path. I made another decision that had the potential to change the course of my life forever.

It was a financial decision that many would have found shocking. I did something that would make Suze Orman's head spin. During one of the most stressful times in business, when money was completely drying up, I decided to take the entire summer off, clear the money out of my retirement account, and use it for freedom and peace.

I realize that this may seem impulsive and irresponsible to some, but for me, it was a necessary step to design a life that works. I had been feeling burnt out and stagnant, and I knew I needed something drastic to shake me out of it.

Did I pay off my bills? No.

Did I spend it on a trip? Nope, not that either.

I invested in something that had been elusive to that point: space for myself. At this point, Elijah, the colicky baby, was now in elementary school and my second child, Jaden, was a toddler. I sent both children to high-quality summer day camps. While they were away during the day, I used the remaining money to live my summer of reflection. I took long walks by myself. I went to the movies almost every day. And I ate delicious, sometimes fancy, food.

In past years, as the summer months approached, I would often get anxious as my attention turned to childcare. Elijah would be home from school. He would need attention, care, and activities. Jaden was a two-year-old toddler, full of energy, who required even more attention. I also needed attention. I was stressed and uncertain about the future. Overwhelmed, I could only think of one solution—space. I needed space to think creatively, to listen to my gut, and to brainstorm how to show up for myself and visualize the kind of life I wanted to deliberately build.

It wasn't always easy, and there were certainly moments of doubt and fear. But with each new experience, I felt more alive and more in tune with my own desires and values. And when I returned home, something had shifted. I felt more grounded, more confident, and sure of my path in life.

When I shared plans of doing this strange "thing," I was told that I was a bit insane and that, as a single mom, this decision was irresponsible. For me, the choice felt right. After talking to several people, only one person thought that this decision was a great idea. This person ended up building a billion-dollar financial services firm. At a lunch with his family and my kids, he said emphatically, "I always prioritize peace and time to think." At a time in my life when it seemed reasonable to hustle and stress, that experience taught me something profound—my improved well-being was directly related to living my values and defining success. I had fun, I thought creatively, and I cherished my freedom. And, on the other side of that, with a clear mind, my company started winning substantial contracts. I reimagined our mission and began a period of rapid growth. My mind overflowed with ideas, and I chased them fearlessly, happily, and proudly. With my head held high, I launched the new iteration of my company knowing that, no matter what happened, I was determined to stay conscious and connected to the things that lead to true riches. I was determined to habitually nurture a life that I *love* and teach others to do the same. Looking back, I can see how all these choices—both big and small—led me to where I am today. Choosing entrepreneurship gave me the freedom and creativity to pursue something meaningful. And choosing to replenish my energy, despite the financial risk, helped me find mental clarity and inner strength.

So if you're at a crossroads in your own life, I encourage you to listen to your heart and take the leap. I am not suggesting that you do what I did. That was my path. It's important to remember that sometimes the journey may not be a big leap. Small steps and tiny deviations from the norm can often lead to unexpected and wonderful outcomes. So be mindful of the middle ground and give yourself time to carefully choose the option that feels right for you.

At the end of the day, it's your unique path, and only you can navigate it. Don't be afraid to take a step back, think things through, and make the best decision for yourself.

Over the years, my company, KUSI Global, has skyrocketed. We currently work with everyone from VPs and presidents of billion-dollar companies to tech-giant CEOs. We conduct trainings with massive, complex organizations, and speak at sold-out events and packed conference halls.

We've helped hundreds of thousands of people turn their businesses—and lives—around. But not through the traditional approaches.

KUSI stands for Knowledge, Understanding, Strategy, and Implementation. It is a human optimization system with a huge mission: to transform humanity through conscious and connected people, leaders, and organizations.

Most leadership books outline a list of strategies to balance budgets, motivate people, communicate effectively, and a host of other tools and tips. Traditional business strategies are missing the most important parts of the journey: customization and consideration of the person behind the strategy. While it is fun to get exact instructions for how to draw a picture, the results are not always as exciting. Imagine what could happen if you had four simple rules that would let you become a Picasso in your field, able to create something abstract with bright colors and bold lines? What if you gained satisfaction from creating, exploring, and teaching a wide variety of styles? What I learned during my summer of reflection differed substantially from traditional advice. That summer, I learned that there are definite secrets to success. We just need to write the playbook on our own terms. No matter which playbook you choose, the ultimate goal remains the same: to climb toward a deeper connection to your power to build a beautiful world.

Climb toward Connection

Without connection, we cease to be truly alive and present in the world. Remember the connective power we had as children, that youthful authenticity that made us laugh with abandon, cry without shame, compliment with sincerity, and love without fear? If you've ever been drawn into conversation with a child as they rambled on about school or play, you know how contagious this type of pure enthusiasm can be—how connected it makes us feel.

How did we lose that kind of primal connection? When did we stop locking eyes with other human beings—strangers or familiar faces—who are chronically delighted to see us? And why? What a profound, aching loss!

So many people around us are trudging through life; their eyes lack passion and light except in the reflected glow of their screens. I talk to so many who share a common feeling in the world today. They feel a bit dull, lost, and concerned about the future. We can bring the light back into the world—and restore our confidence in what we can accomplish together— if we commit to a lifelong journey of connection.

With conscious connections, we aren't driven to reject or accept ourselves and others. We recover quickly from upset and give others the benefit of the doubt. When we make mistakes, we embrace the opportunity to learn and grow, and we extend this grace to others.

Extended to others, conscious connections are the purest form of power—the kind that allows us to live without apology or competition. Not about goals, angles, or manipulation, this inner power motivates us to progress on our leadership journey. It concentrates our potential like that of many historic leaders. We can change minds, change hearts, and lift spirits.

In one of the most memorable and debated speeches of his presidency, Barack Obama stated that supporting our connections with each other may be one of our biggest challenges. "Each of us has a role in fulfilling our common, greater purpose—not merely to seek high position, but to plumb greater depths so that we may find the strength to love more fully."[1]

The true source of change, *love,* begins with *connection.* Connection is true, authentic energy. It is power. It is *not* abstract. When we create understanding within, between, and among our growing connections, we magnify our strength. The result is a conscious connection.

Conscious connection simply reflects a desire to understand humanity and be on the cutting edge of massive changes. We listen in a way that leaves us still. We seem incapable of offending or being offended. We become more interested in how others' experiences have molded them. We see their achievements and failures as adornments—beautiful pieces of who they are.

This book will help you build conscious connections, find pockets of personal bliss, and help save the world. The central philosophy is LOVE, which stands for four interlocking habits:

- Listen

- Observe

- Value

- Engage

If we practice these habits consistently, each of us moves humanity toward the dream of connection. Home, work, and community relationships all become clean canvases ready and positioned for positive change.

LOVE provides the foundation for greatness.

NASA launched a satellite that traveled for ten months to hit an asteroid nearly seven million miles away. Seven million. Imagine the practice and calculations, the theories, and simulations it took to accomplish that task. Missteps and adjustments were all part of that journey. The LOVE system is the technical support for connections—for our lives—creating the same kind of near magic it took to hit a distant rock in space.

By focusing on deepening our ability to LOVE repeatedly, we will collect more power with each effort. Through practice and deliberate action, we can master the four habits. Then, we can generate more influence, joy, happiness, achievement, and meaning in our lives. We may also shoot a rocket or two into space.

This book is about that climb toward connection. We can reach great heights. Denying the world's pain is hollow, but so is obsessing over it. If we fight only to defend our own points of view, our lives will be empty. We may preserve our own identities, but the cost of that preservation is too high—we shut ourselves off from others. We miss the joy of experiencing all the world has to offer.

Through the critical skill of opening our minds and connecting with others, we can move beyond limiting beliefs and strive toward understanding. This is the power of a leader's LOVE, and it allows us to lead with a new sense of purpose.

You will also find that choosing to master and evaluate how you use these habits will trigger your new manifestation machine. Your world will be simple, clear, and full of daily miracles.

In the pages that follow, I'll guide you down the path to becoming more consciously connected to how you experience and impact the world around you. Among the topics we'll cover:

- Why we feel so isolated and alone, even though we're surrounded by constant communication

- What it means to be alive in the world

- Why deep listening is the key to mental health—and how it can make you the smartest person in the room

- How a simple habit of observing reveals the interrelated systems all around us
- Why your interactions with others feel fake and rehearsed
- What it means to engage with others, even when we don't feel we should have to
- How to access the power of conscious connection through the LOVE system to transform how you live and lead—no matter your challenges, desires, or stage in life

Get ready to define your vision for the world and yourself, understand your role, make the necessary mindset shifts, and bask in the warmth of conscious connection.

The Four Habits: Listen, Observe, Value, and Engage

Love is the beginning of the journey, its end, and the journey itself. On the path to love, impossibilities are resolved by turning non-love into love. The love you feel in life is a reflection of the love you feel in yourself. Love is the ultimate truth at the heart of the universe and transcends all boundaries.

—DEEPAK CHOPRA

If you slow down and learn to listen, observe, value, and engage—to LOVE—you can have, do, and be anything you want. You will have the power of conscious connection.

Immerse yourself in the words of history's greatest leaders and feel inspired by their captivating messages. Delve into books filled with stories of transformation, optimism, and progress to gain insight on personal or professional development. These amazing works offer a wealth of knowledge that all comes down to four essential habits.

LOVE is a unified system that keeps us conscious and connected to what matters most. Investing in LOVE brings rewards. By dedicating ourselves to developing daily habits like choosing empowering thought patterns and making wise choices, we can dramatically transform our perspectives on the world around us while maximizing our influence over outcomes.

Love will elevate your thoughts and power. The system will create conscious connections that enrich your life, both professionally and personally. Harness the power of these four essential habits to unlock new potential and transform your life--they will propel you forward, inspiring all other constructive behaviors that take you closer to realizing your dreams.

Learning the LOVE system is simple to remember but takes effort to master. It is mastery that can turn ordinary people into extraordinary visionaries like the great leaders of our time. Don't expect to master each skill overnight—transformation is a journey, not a destination. By prioritizing LOVE on your to-do list, you can clarify what you really need to do in order to live an extraordinary life.

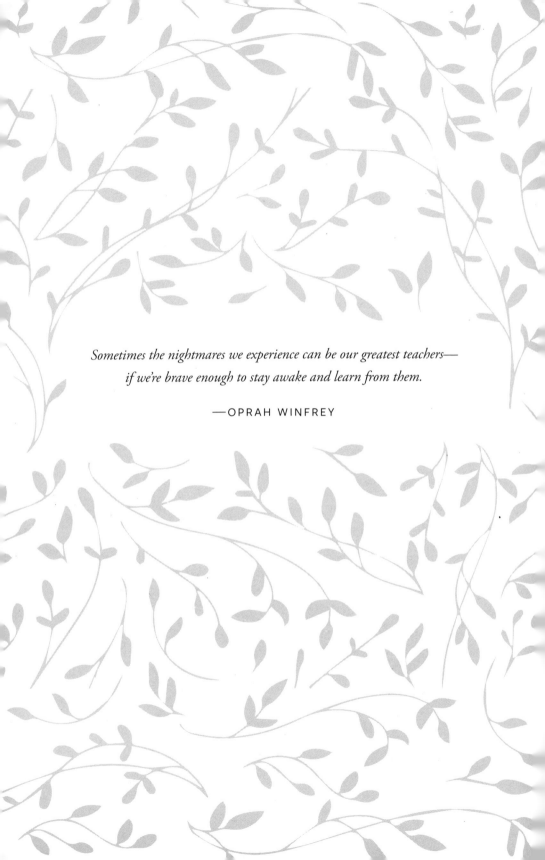

*Sometimes the nightmares we experience can be our greatest teachers—
if we're brave enough to stay awake and learn from them.*

—OPRAH WINFREY

CHAPTER ONE

BREAK FREE FROM THE NIGHTMARE: CHOOSE THE DREAM

Imagine a World . . .

Imagine a world where no one makes eye contact. With no ability to stop and reflect, people plow forward, always busy, always in a hurry. Everything moves so fast that people lose their ability to slow down, too distracted by their pace to connect with anyone else.

You rush down the stairs to the subway, one person amid a horde of zombies. Around you, dozens of heads angle down, glowing blue in the light of their devices. No one looks up, too engrossed in their own little world to notice you. They ignore the shared wonder, beauty, innovation, and life of the collective space.

One man, tall and thin with a spot of razor burn on his neck, clutches a coffee cup in one hand and his phone in the other. Although he's worked at the same location for a decade, he doesn't know the name of the elderly doorman who has worked there even longer. He's never bothered to study the man's face, and he won't even realize when the man is gone one day, replaced by another worker without fanfare.

The woman standing next to him, in her slim black trousers and modestly patterned blouse, has dark circles under her eyes. Dulled and numb, she doesn't even notice the woman right next to her now, a woman she doesn't know, but who has been sitting just three cubicles down from her at work for the past five years. If either had looked up, there still would be no recognition behind their eyes. She doesn't look up, though, fumbling with her purse as she replies, one-handed, to an email.

Sometimes, it feels like we're living a nightmare.

The nightmare of an uncertain economic future.

The nightmare of mass illness and death.

The nightmare of a polarized world. On each side of the divide, morphed into symbolic zombies, we march forward, unfocused and lacking true purpose. The world is made up of individuals concerned only with destroying their opposition and creating more like-minded zombies. Although deceptively quiet, this is a world of shouting. Millions of us scream in anger so loudly that we can't hear others above the clamor. The world's most vulnerable suffer because we've lost the ability to listen. In this nightmare, we ignore others' pain and close ourselves to true connection.

At the heart of the nightmare is a lack of connection. Closed off and trapped, we find ourselves in individual, invisible prisons of our own making. We live on the same planet as billions of unique people, but we overlook other ways of thinking, more concerned with being right than understanding others' emotions or stories.

In this nightmare world, even when we seek connection with others, we do so by expressing our own opinions on social, cultural, and political issues. Our primary concern is defending our own thoughts, even when doing so diminishes other people's humanity. In the nightmare, we talk of integrity, kindness, fairness, and love, but we don't know how to live those values. We lie to ourselves, claiming to honor those values, but not acting on them. We avoid engaging people we perceive as different to protect our own ideals. We're too afraid to hear others, falsely convinced that differing opinions will somehow diminish our status.

This leaves us with a need for clarity about who we are and who we want to be. Instead of the comfort, change, and progress we seek, we find only confusion. Often, our conversations with people who have opposing ideas leave us disappointed. Like a maze with no beginning and no end, we wander aimlessly through the day's talking points, realizing with each passing minute that something is missing.

And, suddenly, we find ourselves in a nightmare of our own making.

Everyday Nightmares

Our choices have the power to shape our identity and the world around us. Small, everyday decisions can form norms and values that become entrenched in our culture and impact every aspect of life—from personal relationships to institutional structures.

When these small behaviors like belittling a colleague for making a mistake become a part of our culture or "way of being," it can create everyday nightmares for everyone. We may not realize how much just one bad decision can reverberate in the short term, but over time they accumulate and manifest into a larger issue that we all suffer from.

Jada is a loving mother. Keeping her son active in music and sports, she provides him with every opportunity for growth and enrichment. Her son should be flourishing. Instead, his grades are well below expectations, and he seems distracted on the soccer field.

Frustrated and angry, Jada puts up with his complaints about soccer practice and homework. School is a constant fight. She endures every parent-teacher conference with a flush of embarrassment, her chest hot with rage as the teacher explains her son's failure to engage.

What is wrong with him? she wonders. *I would have killed for half the opportunities he has. Where have I gone wrong? Why doesn't he appreciate my sacrifices?*

It's easy to spot Jada's error. Too busy pushing her son to fulfill *her* dreams, she fails to connect with him. She can't see that he has a learning disability. She's too distracted to realize that he doesn't like soccer. She can't see his talent for art or his interest in animals. She thinks she has done everything right for her son, but from our outside perspective, we see that she's living a nightmare. Unable to truly see or hear her son's needs, she's a well-intentioned parent—but she lacks the skills to truly listen to her child and observe the impact her decisions have on him.

Jada's situation isn't so different from Maria's.

For seven years, Maria worked hard at her company, giving each task her best effort. But something felt off. As a remote worker, she had grown accustomed to being alone and didn't know how to reintegrate with her colleagues. Despite being surrounded by people in the office, she felt more isolated than ever.

That all changed one day in the cafeteria, when Maria decided to join in on a conversation about a new company policy. She spoke up forcefully, finally sharing her opinion after years of being overlooked and ignored. But to her surprise, her views were met with disdain and ridicule from her coworkers.

It was the most attention Maria had ever received in her work life, but it left her feeling more alone than ever. She had unwittingly triggered a shouting match that brought to light the toxic culture of her workplace. Underneath the veneer of happy smiles and agreement, there was a pervasive silence that prevented authentic connections from forming.

Maria's outburst exposed the truth—that the company's culture promoted avoidance of conflict instead of encouraging healthy, respectful discussions. Rather than connecting and discussing ideas, coworkers engaged in gossip and fake smiles. It was a part of the workplace culture that even new employees quickly learned to participate in.

Suppose leadership at Maria's company was conscious about building culture and worked to connect with the employees enough to identify their needs and develop shared values and expectations. Maria might have found herself armed with the skill to productively express herself. She might have found herself a member of an interdependent team ready to have each other's back. When a team of thinkers sees how their skills, personalities, strengths, and weaknesses work together, they can reach a common goal. She might have found herself part of a more productive whole, grounded in compassion and understanding. There may have been space for civil disagreement, a mutual respect of different opinions.

Like Jada and Maria, Dewayne considers himself a good person. He's active in his church, popular among coworkers, and adored by his wife and kids. When a storm knocks out his power Sunday night, Monday morning arrives too fast. He wakes up late, bolts out of bed, and fumbles through the dark for something to wear. Already late, he stubs his toe and accidentally grabs the leaky coffee thermos. Everything is going wrong.

As Dewayne swerves into the parking lot at work, one eye on the car's clock, a middle-aged woman in a Honda takes the spot he'd been eyeing. "You idiot!" he yells through the windshield. "Learn to drive!" As she gets out of her car, he stares her down, willing her to look his way. When she does, he flips her off. To him, she is just an inconvenient obstacle— someone who took *his* parking spot.

To her family, she is a single mother fighting hard for her kids, and she's just been diagnosed with early-stage breast cancer.

Dewayne couldn't see beyond his own needs and losses. Dewayne was not conscious of his behavior or connected to its impact on others.

Most of us like to think we would never behave like Dewayne. Like him, we think of ourselves as good people. When we're disconnected and we focus on ourselves, it's easy to overlook other people's struggles.

Like the others, Tony doesn't always get things right.

As the director of a local homeless shelter, he's passionate about his work. He's so passionate, in fact, that he demands perfection from everyone around him. A poor communicator, Tony rarely explains his expectations, and when the organization's volunteers and employees fall short—as teams often do—he diminishes their efforts and treats them like obstacles in his path to success. He forgets that, without them, he could accomplish nothing. Under his leadership, fundraising efforts sputter, meal servers miss their shifts, and office staff turnover is higher than it's ever been. Tony simply can't understand it. He values integrity above all else, and he knows his workers want to help the people they serve. But the harder he pushes, the worse things get. His demands for excellence result in just the opposite.

Most of us know people like Tony, and many of us can relate to him. Yet, when we look at the situation objectively, it's easy to see what's happening. He isn't really connecting with his workers, so his pushing only results in stress, anxiety, and burnout. Although he sees himself as selfless, his need to succeed overrides his concern for others around him. His lack of true engagement has caused Tony to lose his most valuable resource—community.

It's easy to judge Jada, Maria, Dewayne, and Tony. If we're honest with ourselves, though, we've all struggled with similar issues. Jada failed to listen. Maria failed to observe. Dewayne failed to value others. And Tony failed to engage with his team. These habits—listening, observing, valuing, and engaging—drive our ability to connect with others. Without them, we not only fail to support others, but we also fail to achieve our own goals.

Our behavior and habits can turn us into zombies, ignoring life, rejecting uniqueness, denying problems, and forgetting to look up and gain clarity about how we choose to live. The nightmare is real when we are not conscious and connected to something bigger. Yet, as with all nightmares, you can wake up. With a little shift, you can step back into the light to realize that you aren't really in danger. You just need to experience more conscious connection. Conscious connection ensures that the nightmare does not define our lives; instead, we come together and choose compassion over ignorance, understanding over misunderstanding, acceptance over rejection, and unity over division. We find ourselves living in an environment where every human being feels valued and safe. We create something beautiful! We build bridges of love, understanding, and peace.

In his revolutionary book *Homo Deus: A Brief History of Tomorrow*, Yuval Noah Harari suggests that our species has come a long way, and it is important to reflect on that journey to create a better future.[1] According to Harari, "We have managed to provide humanity with food, shelter, and security, and we have eradicated many of the diseases that once plagued us." However, there are still crucial issues that need to be addressed as a society. Harari believes that "it is up to us to decide the kind of future we want to create." We need to take steps, both big and small, to make a difference. As Harari notes, "Even the smallest action can have an enormous impact." By doing so, we can leave a positive legacy for future generations.

As we work toward a brighter future, it is essential to keep in mind how small decisions can create big changes. Even interactions that may seem trivial offer us the chance to build deeper connections. Our interactions with others give us great power and the opportunity to make a difference. Every choice we make, no matter how small it may seem, can lead to a positive or negative outcome. We must strive to use our power wisely and create something truly remarkable by embracing the little decisions that shape our future and collective destiny. Together we have the courage and strength to achieve the extraordinary! With every step, let's remember that our choices have an immeasurable impact on what kind of world we live in. By joining together with purpose and determination, we can create something beautiful that will last far into the future.

Living the Dream: An Exercise

The first step in mastering this system is to find opportunities to LOVE (listen, observe, value, engage) in your everyday life. Below I'll offer some examples of genuine connection. As you read, think about examples from your own life and picture yourself helping create a positive conscious connection in the situations you encounter each day.

Dream with Others

Pat could not begin to express his elation and satisfaction in seeing his mentee, Jay, promoted to a higher position than his own. Jay was talented, intelligent, and ready. It was as though Pat experienced his mentee's promotion as his own.

> Who is the Pat in your world? Do you have a friend, colleague, or loved one eager to share your joy? Can you picture yourself in Pat's place? What barriers stand in your way to observing others' joy and success? How can you uplift the Jays in your life?

Dream for Others

In the heat of a harsh Arizona summer, a coffee shop drive-through is overtaken by generosity as a seemingly never-ending train of cars keeps paying for the bill of the car in their rearview mirror.

> What would it feel like to be in this situation? How would it make you feel about others in the drive-through line? In what ways can you acknowledge the value of others without expecting something in return? How can you bring joy to someone else today? What small acts of kindness can you offer the world?

Dream for the World

Jasmine, Latonya, Sarah, and Michaela are all 15-year-olds who dream of changing the world. Through social media, they see people who are really making a difference in social justice. While they are too young to participate in protest directly, they gather their parents and grandparents for an informal forum—they want to share their own perspectives on the day's issues and learn about previous generations' worldviews. The open and honest conversation helps everyone understand each other better.

> What social issues are important to you? How can you engage others and educate yourself on those issues? What can you share to bring people together? Can you get involved with causes you find important? What questions do you have about others' perspectives? How might you learn about different worldviews? Are you open to listening? Are you open to change?

Dream for Change

A billion-dollar corporation hires Camila, an award-winning scientist with more than 25 years of experience. Camila gets excited when her team members share new ideas, innovations, and perspectives. She revels in the evolution of the human mind and works hard to set her ego aside. Secure in who she is, she celebrates her team's brilliance and gets excited about developing other award-winning scientists whom she can learn from.

How can you celebrate others' innovations and accomplishments, particularly in an area where you excel? Are there people in your everyday life who would truly value the simple act of being heard or acknowledged? In what ways can you use your skills, education, or organizational power to recognize the contributions of others? What voices need to be heard on your team?

Dreaming of a Connected World

I think you would be shocked at all the challenges that the daily practice of LOVE can solve. For one, effectively using these skills requires a lifelong journey of continuous improvement. Finding ways to practice LOVE throughout our day can lead to a monumental shift in ourselves, others, and the world.

Throughout this book, I'll encourage you to start a chain reaction that causes that shift. As you practice incorporating LOVE into your everyday encounters, you inspire others to do the same. Your journey toward LOVE will be fun, engaging, and highly entertaining. It may sometimes feel like you're not making progress. Meaningful connections often require silence so you can listen, patience to observe, and reflection on your values before making conscious choices.

The LOVE system is your cheat sheet for life and a rule book for working through some of your most complex challenges. By reflecting on the questions in the "Living the Dream" exercise above as a daily practice, you have begun your own journey toward ending the nightmare, living the dream, and learning to LOVE.

No single person can change the world. That's why this book is focused on connection. Through connection, we can help others. Through connection, we can accept others and share their enthusiasm. Through connection, we can celebrate others' uniqueness and move beyond challenging issues to a world of unlimited possibilities for our future. Through connection, we can imagine a world where people live their values every day, even in the face of differences.

Relief for Us All

My heart broke for the first time in third grade. It wasn't an unrequited childhood crush or a broken friendship. It was the kind of broken heart that comes from realizing that hurt people hurt other people.

I watched as my father straightened the collar of his freshly pressed uniform.

"Cable guy at your service," he said into the mirror, with hesitant enthusiasm, struggling to mask his Bahamian accent. I'd never seen my father in a uniform or even known him to have a job. As a matter of fact, I usually never saw him during the day. He was a musician—a drum-playing, loud-talking night owl, overflowing with excitement and big dreams. After growing up with dozens of brothers and sisters, he taught himself to read, and he mastered the art of percussion.

I'm not sure how much I knew about my dad back then, but I knew without a doubt that he was an entertainer, and a darn good one—"true and true," as they say on the island.

That day, though, he dressed in his uniform and prepared to fix other families' cable. It became a fixture of my childhood memories. That day, he looked me square in the eye and said, "Kings must do tings demselves sometimes." Then, he yelled, "I's a king!" and belted out his laugh, always larger than life.

I don't know what led him to his new job, but I remember being startled. Frankly, I thought he was losing his mind. And yet he had such a great attitude. He even promised to take me to a fancy restaurant to celebrate his first day. I was so excited!

In our moderately embarrassing old white van, he pulled up to the restaurant and parked the car. His nametag, I suddenly realized, said "Bill." *That isn't his name*, I thought. His hand clutched mine, and I noticed it was ashy. Usually soaked in strong cologne and clean-shaven, with a slight shine to his hair, he looked different that day.

We walked through the double doors of the restaurant. The smell of grilled meat hit me, and I remember feeling extra excited to have a meal with my dad. My father walked up to the hostess stand and asked for a table. The hostess did not respond. She kept her head down and seemed engrossed in the details of the table chart. He asked again with a bit more bass in his voice. She looked right past him and helped the people behind us instead. He asked one more time and was completely ignored. My father took my little hand and started walking toward the exit. I could tell he was upset because he started clearing his throat. When he did this, it was usually followed by a statement that reflected his philosophy in life, "Everyting cool." He decided to swallow the offense and politely leave. At that moment, I felt sad, then got angry. I was only eight years old, but like my dad, I developed my own philosophy. A deep feeling in my gut led me to two words.

"That's enough!"

I realized then that I had an edge that my father did not. I could communicate with power and clarity at the tender age of eight.

"I'd like to speak with the manager," I said.

I stood on my tippy toes and spoke in what I called my "adult voice." I told the manager what happened and that I would have to let the world know how this restaurant treated us. He apologized profusely, sat us in the best seat in the house, and took care of the bill for our meal. I was satisfied and oh-so-pleased.

As I looked into my dad's eyes, I saw something else. I saw a grown man in pain. Though he tried hard to smile, he couldn't mask that something was wrong. His eight-year-old daughter had to stand up for him. I don't remember many details of the evening, but I'll never forget the feeling.

I'd won. And I'd also lost.

My desire for justice morphed into compassion as I realized how downright mean the world can be. I wished my father didn't have to feel shame, and somehow, I felt sad for the hostess, too. I realized that she also had to deal with the moment's discomfort.

This experience planted a seed in my heart. I vowed to help others increase their power through empathy and compassion. This can only happen if we listen and see each other. At eight years old, I realized that everyone in the restaurant was sad, and I wanted relief for us all. No one knew how to find it.

Even in my early years, I yearned to walk into a room and feel powerful and important. I lived life aware of the contrast between how people looked at me and how they looked at others. I felt the judgment, the shame, and the constant struggle to achieve something that would, one day, make me feel good enough. I didn't know exactly what that meant. My dream was to simply earn enough money for a house with an organized closet and a couple of golden retrievers. The vision morphed over time, but the intention was the same. I had to be great at *something*. Anything. And from that greatness, I wanted to be seen. I would protect those who feel oppressed as they try to find a voice in the world.

When we reject oppression, we open ourselves up to a world of possibilities. Life is a series of moments and interactions, each one having the potential to be an opportunity for personal growth. By paying attention to who we encounter along our journey and learning from them, we can discover enlightening Insights about ourselves. We discover our power to create meaningful change. We give ourselves the opportunity to create something better and more equitable. We can use our own power and strength to build bridges, not walls; to work against injustice, instead of perpetuating it; and to make sure that everyone is heard, seen, and valued. What will happen if we don't break down the barriers that prevent us from living in harmony with each other? When we refuse to acknowledge the effects of our choices on others and disregard our interconnectedness, life can quickly become a living nightmare.

Are you able to observe the world with compassion? Are you attuned to possibilities for transformation? The incident at the restaurant with my father was a moment of revelation. Microaggressions, as I came to understand, are subtle, often unintentional offenses directed at a minority or nondominant group, which tend to reinforce harmful stereotypes.

Microaggressions can be tricky to identify and deal with, as they are often subtle in nature and easily overlooked. However, when we pay attention to ourselves, others, and the world, we gain a heightened understanding of the full picture. We can better navigate and address microaggressions. Instead of being driven by ignorance, we are motivated by a desire to understand and connect.

It's important to understand the power dynamics at play when microaggressions occur—and know when it's appropriate to take a stand or step back. We can all be allies for those who are affected by microaggressions through our voices, self-awareness, empathy, and compassionate action. It's essential that we equip ourselves with strategies for coping with the impacts of these types of insults so that we can move forward and impact change.

When faced with injustice or discrimination, exercise strategic restraint by practicing LOVE before taking action. Listen deeply, understand diverse perspectives, and consider power dynamics. Then, let your values guide your choices. Pause for LOVE to use your voice responsibly, while creating a space to elevate the goal to something that results in growth and expansion for everyone.

With practice, we get better at using our power and our voice to take a stand or to stand down. How do you know when you did the right thing? Well, it feels a bit like love and relief. Only you can know.

The Solution: More Conscious and Connected People Practicing Four Simple Habits

The lessons in this book come from years of LOVE (listen, observe, value, engage) with people from all walks of life. My role has many titles: motivator, trainer, teacher, leadership strategist, diversity strategist, researcher, writer, speaker, life coach, and guide. I've assisted leaders in developing innovative strategies for some of the most critical and complex missions globally including defense, wealth inequalities, racial and social justice, aviation, and health care. By leveraging strategic intelligence and by fostering connected cultures and conscious equity,* I help organizations maximize human potential.

These accomplishments describe my work but fall short of communicating who I am. While a bit funny—perhaps too goofy for some—I prefer a different set of terms: lovebug, lover, connector, heart-tugger, destiny-tickler, or perhaps a long and complex description as an unapologetic revolutionizer of the human condition. Too far? Maybe. Close to my heart, these all speak to my experience and approach. And they demonstrate how I strive to keep the heart present during hardcore business strategy.

I began exploring the principles of what I now call *conscious connection* as a counseling psychologist. I sought to improve the cultural competence of therapists in underserved communities. I was drawn to two therapeutic philosophies: cognitive behavioral therapy (CBT) and existential approaches. CBT supports behavior change by addressing faulty or unhelpful thought patterns. How do your thoughts impact your choices? Existential approaches to life seek to soothe anxiety by grounding our focus in a search for purpose and authenticity. What is my purpose? Who am I? Early in my career, I connected these two approaches to leadership.

---

*Equity is a critical aspect of diversity, inclusion, and social justice work. "Conscious Equity" is the process of actively striving for equity in our organizations and communities by incorporating systems thinking, cultural intelligence, and emotional intelligence into our leadership approaches.

At KUSI Global, the Conscious Equity training track focuses on developing personal capacity and deepening self-awareness to help leaders turn awareness into action. By understanding how equity intersects with power dynamics and privilege, we can better recognize how our individual behaviors contribute to creating or reinforcing inequities—and work to dismantle them. It's important for leaders to be conscious about equity by recognizing their power and identifying ways they can use it to support marginalized groups.

By bringing together these two philosophies, conscious connection became a driving goal to empower individuals to become more self-aware and make decisions that align with their core values. The goal is to help individuals realize their full potential by unlocking the power of conscious thought and action. By gaining knowledge of our own reflections and experiences, as well as those around us, we can make decisions that result in collective gains. We get everything we want. We connect authentically with ourselves and others from a place of openness and understanding. And we feel a genuine sense of belonging and joy that naturally follows. This is the kind of experience that conscious connection creates.

The principles of conscious connection and the LOVE habits contain the core principles I've learned through connecting with real people on their journeys. I have sat with homeless veterans and listened to their stories. I have coached professors at prestigious universities. I have led programs at billion-dollar companies. I've worked with tech giants, large government agencies, law firms, banks, insurance companies, religious institutions, large health-care companies, and higher education. I have taught employees and leaders with decades of public service. I have listened to valuable stories from citizens returning from prison, high-level executives transitioning into retirement, and middle managers climbing the ranks of their organizations.

And I worked with children impacted by HIV and AIDS. There, I discovered the role of consciousness in communicating about pain and loss—those moments when our feelings are so intense that we have to stop and just breathe. In the small, quaint, homey row house where I worked, children came to feel a sense of belonging. I met a lot of kids there, but three of them had an unforgettable impact on my soul.

The first was a 15-year-old boy with a sweet spirit and a faint smile. Each day, he came to the center and tried so hard to be like the other kids, but he was often too physically sick to participate fully. I visited him in hospice days before he took his last breath. Then there was a 12-year-old boy with both learning and physical disabilities. He refused to use the assistance of leg braces or allow his friends to help him. He preferred to limp around the house on his own. I sat with him as he wrote rap lyrics about his life. Finally, there was a 17-year-old girl who sang like an angel. She seemed normal on all fronts but had a backstory that took my breath away. Her dreams, confidence, and hope for something better were infectious. I cried with her when she got into college.

The opportunity to connect with those children brought me gratitude on most days. On other days, I held my own son tight as I gasped at the horror of their stories. They'd experienced suffering, death, loss, broken promises, sickness, sacrifice, homelessness, and fear—all before adulthood. However, they also shared stories of hope, joy, and love. I was conscious of a complex connection that gave me both purpose and pause.

As I continued my search for a "pocket of purpose" connected to this experience, I became obsessed with how power could both ease pain and increase joy. With other clients, I saw how treatments were affected when doctors failed to listen, observe, and make connections to the complicated challenges that impacted their outcomes. Instructions to "Take this medication three times a day with food" assume that food is available three times per day. When doctors asked patients if they were taking their meds regularly, they often looked down in shame and whispered, "No." One doctor confided in me that "these kinds of patients" often lack discipline. Through listening, observing, valuing strengths, and asking questions, I was able to work with patients and care teams to address shame and ensure that bellies were full so meds would not cause nausea.

When medical professionals fail to pay close attention to minor behavioral changes, they could make deadly mistakes. Rushing through their visits—forgetting their reason for serving patients—could be a matter of life or death. When they took the time to really engage with the people that needed them, they could change and save their lives.

My work in the nonprofit sector opened my eyes to the power of leadership. I realized that having strong leadership skills can be a formidable force. They can foster progress and allow us to witness drastic and minor evolution within the people around us and within ourselves.

I began using the LOVE system as a strategy to demonstrate a new version of competence to those who often felt overlooked and unheard. I became both strategic and conscious about my connection to the solution.

I realized then that LOVE can literally be a matter of life or death.

Waking Up

I began this chapter by describing a nightmare. Crowded with symbolic zombies, that world was terrible—but, for most of us, it was also very familiar.

With LOVE, we can imagine a different world. This time, the morning subway is a hustle and bustle of community—a shared space, a common story, a collective energy leveraged to uplift everyone. No longer zombies, these commuters are a new kind of humanity. Their eyes are bright as they search for connection, full of gratitude and bliss. They are captivated by differences. They are inspired by the world around them. And they live to change the world for the better.

TAKEAWAYS

In this chapter, we've opened the door to understanding what it means to be consciously connected and how to get there.

What can a massive wave of people committed to these skills turned habits do for you and the world? We can restore the integrity and beauty of the human experience. Together, we can escape what feels like a nightmare, imagine a new world, and invite opportunities to accomplish our individual and collective dreams.

Here are a few key points to remember as you read on:

- **We all yearn to be heard.** The first step in becoming truly connected is realizing that everyone longs for that connection, and if we achieve it, we will live our most fulfilling lives.

- **We are more powerful than we know.** Once we've acknowledged the need for connection, we must realize that we have the power to create it and derive even more power from it.

- **Conscious connection requires us to be present,** conscious of, and connected to things that elevate our power to shape our destiny and impact the world.

- **We are often blinded by our own struggles.** Our lives are complex, filled with trials and triumphs, and we can become so focused on ourselves that we forget that others are living equally complex lives. Open your mind to consider others' experiences.

- **Wake up from the nightmare.** To become fully present, we must LOVE. Listen to yourself and those around you, observe the world and the people in it, value yourself and others, and put all of that into practice by being fully engaged.

The LOVE System

*Love, habits, and connections are the most
powerful human creations.
They can transform lives and create a world
of meaning out of chaos.*

—IRVIN D. YALOM

LOVE represents a system of habits that will transform how you live and lead.

Listening builds emotional intelligence.
Listening improves mental health.

Observation sharpens systems thinking.
Observation supports confident decision-making.

Aligned values support cultural competence (intelligence).
Clear values in action improve happiness and well-being.

Engagement is critical to effective communication.
Engagement supports personal success
and healthy relationships.

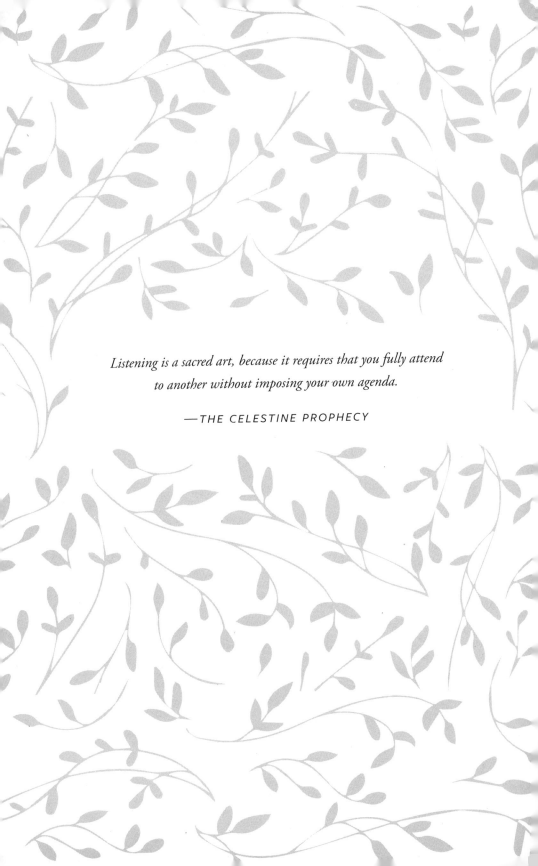

*Listening is a sacred art, because it requires that you fully attend
to another without imposing your own agenda.*

—THE CELESTINE PROPHECY

CHAPTER TWO

LISTEN

Listen to Be Well

The faint whiff of cigarettes trickled through the back window along with a burst of unapologetic laughter.

"Man!" Uncle Barry exclaimed to no one in particular. "Whatdya mean?"

As though drawn to his chaotic energy, I wandered back to the corner of the dining room and gazed out at him. He must have sensed me coming because he turned to face me and winked through the window.

"Hey, Tally," he said, his voice rich and smooth, resonant and charming as a seasoned DJ.

"Hey, Uncle Barry," I returned. He'd already turned away from me, taking a drag from the shrinking Newport.

After a big family dinner, my stomach was full and happy. We'd all loaded our plates from heaping dishes of collard greens, macaroni and cheese, candied yams, and turkey, then crowded around my great-grandmother's antique table. It had been a true exercise in willpower not to go back for seconds, but as Uncle Neil pointed out, just one helping left more room for my famous sweet potato pie.

Now, after we'd left the table, some collapsing on the couch and others chatting in the kitchen, Uncle Barry snuffed his cigarette on the cement floor of the porch. I slipped through the iron bars blocking the entrance to the door to join him outside.

"Hey, Tally," he repeated, our earlier exchange seemingly forgotten.

"Hey, Uncle Barry."

We stood there for a moment, the quiet of the afternoon marked only by the kids' squeals.

Jamming his hand in his pocket, he pulled out his pack of cigarettes and smacked the base against the heel of his hand. His strong shoulders and narrow hips silhouetted against the late afternoon sun, he held an unlit cigarette between his lips and clicked his lighter. Something about the way he moved reminded me of the smooth, sweeping movements of an outfielder in mid-throw.

He could have been a great baseball player. Known for his skill and grace on the baseball field, Barry was the kid everybody liked—handsome, popular, and smart. He was going places.

Then, in his early 20s, he got restless.

He would rise in the middle of the night and trudge down the stairs to the street. Guided by some unseen, indescribable urge, he strolled down Atlantic Avenue in Brooklyn, New York, and sauntered through its busiest intersection. Late-night drivers must have gawked as he continued toward the railroad station, picking up speed as he approached the next borough. Still he marched on, into the dark, lonely, quiet of night.

Except the night wasn't quiet—not for Barry. And neither was our shared afternoon on the front porch of our family's Brooklyn brownstone.

In his early 20s, strange, disembodied voices stole his peace. His mind was flooded with them, and nobody could figure out where they came from.

In response, he wandered and paced, searching for something.

I wondered, as I watched him pacing and smoking on the porch that day, what he'd been looking for.

"Hey, Tally," he said again. "Do you know Sam Cooke?"

To a casual observer, the question might have seemed strange. What brought the famous singer and Civil Rights activist to my uncle's mind? Why ask whether I know him?

The question didn't surprise me at all. In fact, I expected it. The exchange followed a familiar pattern, a conversation he and I share every time we see each other.

I nodded. "Sure do."

"You better know him!" he laughed.

As he turned on his heel, flinging open the heavy door to the house, I knew he'd gone to pour a cup of coffee. Uncle Barry's routine was as predictable as it was simple. He'd smoke, have a quick conversation, grab a cup of coffee, and repeat the whole thing again.

No matter how many times I answer, he never seems to process my response. The voices have formed an impenetrable fortress around his mind. Nobody can break through. He must want to connect with others. Friendly and silly, he always loved to tease me. He continues to call me by my childhood nickname Tally, which I've never quite been able to shake.

My words can't reach him. Drowned out by the voices that invaded his mind all those years ago, my speech is like an inaudible whisper to him.

I've never denied him the Sam Cooke conversation, and I never will. Even though his wandering never brought him closer to me, I can still feel him searching, trying to connect through the noise inside his mind.

During a fleeting moment of his lucidity, I asked him once, "Uncle Barry, how do people treat you?"

"They're afraid of me," he answered, "so some people bother me and throw rocks at me if I get too close to them."

"Do you know why?" I asked, hoping to prolong our chat before the inevitable cup of coffee.

His response rocked my soul.

"My mind is gone," he said. "But nothing is wrong with my heart."

He stayed with me for one more second. Then, busting out a rendition of Sam Cooke's hit, "You Send Me," he grabbed his mug and headed out to smoke.

Sometimes I wonder whether he remembers how he used to be. Back then, he effortlessly connected with friends, family, and girls at school—to hear my Uncle Neil, his younger brother, tell it, he connected with everyone he met.

That's more than most of us can say.

I often wonder what his life is like in his care facility. When he wanders the street, where does he go? I wonder if his long walks and pacing are his body's way of searching for connection. Or searching for what Uncle Barry might have lost—the ability to be conscious and connected. He lost the capacity to fully listen and engage.

What are you searching for? Have you found it?

"You Know Sam Cooke?"

My uncle Barry was diagnosed with schizophrenia* years ago. While his mental illness seemed to rob him of his ability to hold full conversations with others, his struggle to listen is far from unique.

Every single day I encounter conversations like the one we shared that day—the one we'd shared many times before—all response, no connection. I meet people who are heartsick over their sense of isolation and loneliness. Wandering through life, searching for connection.

"Why won't people respect me?" they ask.

"Why doesn't anybody care about my ideas?"

I can almost see the fortress they've built around their minds. Like a door slammed shut to everyone around them, they've closed themselves off from the true path to wisdom.

"You know Sam Cooke?" they may as well ask.

---

* Neurodiversity describes the idea that people experience and interact with the world around them in different ways. There is no one "right" way of thinking, learning, and behaving. Differences are not viewed as deficits. For more, see Nicole Baumer and Julia Frueh, "What Is Neurodiversity?" on the Harvard Health Publishing website: https://www.health.harvard.edu/blog/what-is-neurodiversity-202111232645.

Diversity experts in the workplace advocate for leaders to establish systems that accommodate diverse needs. It is well known that many people with schizophrenia can both function and excel in multiple functions, including very demanding jobs. This illness impacts people differently. And the side effects and consistency of medication play a role in one's capacity to function.

My uncle Barry's case is not a reflection of all people diagnosed with this illness. The skill of listening assumes one's capacity to make cognitive behavioral changes to choices. If you suspect that you have chronic focus issues or find it extremely challenging to listen or tame your thoughts, explore resources to get additional support. A part of connecting consciously is being able to gauge when a behavior requires support beyond your own internal resources. The skill of listening presumes that individuals possess the mental and behavioral flexibility to make adjustments.

When I speak with these people, I wonder how much time they waste asking the same questions over and over. I wonder whether they realize how closed off they are. If they stand on their porch on a quiet afternoon, do they hear children playing, or do they hear an off-kilter orchestra, the noise of their own minds drowning out everyone and everything around them?

At least Uncle Barry *knows* he struggles to listen.

As I've traveled the country, speaking with tens of thousands of people, I've recognized my uncle's struggles in people with all kinds of backgrounds, skills, accolades, and titles.

Many of us remain confident in our ability to listen, insisting that we've been doing so all our lives. We believe we should focus our leadership efforts on other, less common skills, gravitating to things that seem newer and more innovative.

Listening is the single most important way to improve our relationships, build community, and achieve our goals. Conscious and connected listening is more complex than it may seem—often, when we think we're listening, we're actually just waiting for the chance to share the voices in our heads.

The difference is crucial—and it changes everything.

The Resume and the Hard Stop

One of the most enthusiastic clients I'd met in some time, Marcus, came to me hoping for guidance. He served as a senior leader for a large government agency for a little over 22 years. His well-tailored suit gave him the confident air of a leader, and his close-cropped hair revealed a healthy degree of care for his appearance. More than that, though, his charming smile and charismatic style made him a perfect fit for his new career venture: motivational speaking.

I arranged for him to meet my colleague, Keisha. A seasoned executive herself, she knew the speaking industry well and offered regular paid consulting for people like Marcus. This meeting was on the house.

As we made our way into her office, Marcus radiated excitement.

"Remember," I said, "she's got a hard stop at 2:15. So keep an eye on the clock."

"Got it!" he confirmed, his words sharp and decisive.

After I'd quickly introduced them, I sat back to observe the conversation. It wasn't much of a conversation at all.

As the minutes ticked by, he spouted a line-by-line rundown of his resume, followed by a laundry list of topics he felt qualified to speak on.

I glanced up at the clock. 1:42. Gesturing animatedly, he circled back to a forgotten line on his resume, chuckling an apology for skipping it.

"No need to apologize," Keisha interjected. "But did you want to talk about—"

"Yes!" he interrupted, nodding vigorously. He leaned forward, placing his elbows on his knees, his index fingers pressed together in a tight triangle.

I breathed a sigh of relief for him, hopeful that her gentle prompting would nudge him toward the purpose of the conversation—to gather information from an experienced professional whose path could help him to forge his own way in the industry.

Instead, he launched back into his resume, this time focusing on his educational accomplishments.

She leaned back in her chair, a pitying expression on her face, and checked her watch.

I glanced at the clock, too. 1:49.

A few moments later, he reached into his bag and retrieved a document. He slid it across her desk. Flashing a bright smile, he explained, "My strategic plan—just a draft, for now."

He read through the document, finishing his explanation at 10 minutes after two. Looking up at her expectantly, he remarked, "I'm really looking forward to this new phase in my life."

She looked almost startled by his conclusion but pressed on. "Well," she offered. "We have about five minutes. Did you have any questions for me?"

In response, he briefly reiterated his plans. "Well, I am really trying to just get my first speaking gig, then plan to build upon that."

"That's great," she said, her eyebrows furrowed slightly. "Thanks for sharing this. I've got to get to my next meeting, but feel free to email me with any questions."

She seemed confused, and I understood why. After watching the meeting as a third-party observer, I had no idea why he'd wanted to meet with her. He learned nothing about her, her skills, her career path, her experiences, or her perspective.

In short, he accomplished nothing. A complete waste of time.

Yet, when I asked him how he felt about the meeting, he replied, "I think it went well!"

It was almost heartbreaking to watch his enthusiasm. Marcus was extremely enthusiastic. When he told me he wanted to learn more about being a motivational speaker, he meant it. So why did he ramble on, turning an amazing networking opportunity into a poorly prepared soliloquy starring his resume?

The answer is both simple and incredibly common. He couldn't quiet the voices in his mind. I suspect that he was anxious and focused on what he was getting out of the relationship. He made a series of classic errors. His insecurity about his path led him to grapple with inner conflicts dominated by ego and pride. Consequently, he became self-absorbed, overlooking chances to contribute. Instead of letting anxiety or a sense of neediness overwhelm you, use these feelings as catalysts to explore how you can add value. In doing so, you'll discover hope, answers, and the emotional support you crave. Prioritize listening, observing, valuing, and engaging to achieve value-based outcomes and expand possibilities.

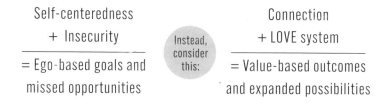

Self-centeredness + Insecurity = Ego-based goals and missed opportunities

Instead, consider this:

Connection + LOVE system = Value-based outcomes and expanded possibilities

Computer, Computer, Computer

It's the end of the quarter and your accounting team emails you a series of documents to review. Along with the usual spreadsheets, they've attached a few charts and flagged several pages for attention. For the most part, your task is to compare the numbers to your company's expected outcomes and goals. Seems simple enough.

On an average afternoon, this might take you an hour or two. You'd sit down with a cup of coffee and a pen—maybe a stack of sticky notes if you really want to get fancy—and move through the charts, line by line, interpreting what you see. Based on your experience with the task, you'd probably narrate the process, making sense of the reports by silently, intuitively talking to yourself.

Now imagine someone asked you to complete that task with one caveat—while you do, you must repeat the word "computer," out loud, over and over again. How do you think you would do? How invested would you feel in the task? How frustrated?

Researchers at the University of Toronto can tell you exactly how well you would perform under these conditions.[1] The researchers gave participants a button marked "go" and seated them in front of a computer screen. When the participant saw a yellow square, they were told to press "go". They were told *not* to press the button if the square was purple. Every few minutes, they saw a screen instructing them to reverse the rule—now purple meant go but yellow didn't. Some participants were allowed to complete the task as presented. Others were given additional instructions—they were told to repeat the word "computer" over and over.

Surprisingly, participants who repeated the word responded 12.5 percent faster than those who completed the task silently. But they did a *terrible* job. They messed up almost 50 percent more often than those who were quiet.

So, what was it about repeating a word aloud that made participants more impulsive and less accurate? According to Drs. Tullett and Inzlicht, the answer isn't about speaking.[2]

It's about listening.

The reason they had participants repeat a word over and over is that doing so blocks out their inner guidance. Left to simply press a button, we can talk ourselves through the task: *Okay, yellow square, go. Oops, no, that was purple. Focus. Keep your eye on the yellow.*

When we are forced to think about other things, we lose access to that inner reasoning. And suddenly, we start messing up. A lot.

As it turns out, you don't have to mumble the same word over and over to experience these results. Most of us find other ways to drown out our voices of reason.

The zombie who speeds to work, weaving in and out of traffic, honking and shouting, repeats, *Late for work, late for the meeting, too late to grab a coffee, late, late, late.*

The zombie who can't get along with his coworkers, who dismisses his support staff as incompetent, repeats, *Everybody lets me down, nobody thinks like me, everything is up to me, me, me, me.*

The zombie on the subway with his nose in his phone repeats, *Bad news in the* WSJ, *bad news from Washington, bad news from my kids' school, bad, bad, bad.*

No wonder they all make such terrible choices. And, as with the participants in this study, life feels frustrating and hard. Without our inner guidance, we become impulsive. Irritable. And our results suffer.

Listening to your inner guidance is different from speaking all your thoughts. The conscious and connected internal voice reflects our values. It reminds us of our purpose. Here is what quality inner guidance might sound like:

I'm curious about unexpected connections and new possibilities.

I judge my progress by how my choices align with my values or impact others.

I accept happiness as a worthy goal.

I open my ears. I challenge my mind.

I am excited about opportunities to move about the world with other people.

I stay focused on the task at hand; I can search for those shoes on Amazon later.

I am not in danger just because someone has a new approach. I can breathe and listen to their ideas.

In the case of Marcus, it might have sounded like: *Let me learn more about Keisha and her journey.*

Like my uncle Barry, we cannot listen if we are constantly drowning in a sea of unconscious voices. In fact, one definition of mental illness is the inability to get out of our own heads. We can get trapped there, overthinking, scolding ourselves, judging others, or cycling through the negative possibilities in our future. At the extreme end of this spectrum is my uncle Barry, whose mental illness has progressed such that he hears other voices besides his own.

You don't have to hear voices to struggle with mental health. Simply feeling trapped in our own minds is a symptom of anxiety, depression, and a host of other common mental health hurdles.

Most people believe listening comes naturally. But when we think of things this way, it makes it clear why so many struggle to truly listen.

True listening requires focus—we must stop that repeating word in our mind before we can really listen to ourselves or others. Beyond simply nodding and blurting out a response, listening requires us to open ourselves to emotions and ideas, slowing our thoughts down so we can truly consider the right path forward.

A master of art, science, or sports practices the physical movements of one's craft repeatedly. Masters train their minds to focus on the task at hand and drown out thoughts and distractions that kick them out of a flow state. Flow state is that place where you are doing something, and your mind is so still that your body seems to have turned the task at hand into something as natural as breathing. This state seems to unlock some of our greatest abilities. A worthy goal is to practice flow state when listening and connecting with others so we can be completely immersed in the experience.

A worthy goal is to practice flow state when listening and connecting with others so we can be completely immersed in the experience.

According to Toronto researchers, deep purposeful listening is not just about connecting with others. It is also about being conscious of what we're doing and increasing the likelihood of better awareness, choices, and results.

Listening is the foundation of mental health and the portal to wisdom. When we quiet our minds, we can truly take in the world around us—and examine the inner world we are creating.

In solitude, we give ourselves the power to discern, understand, and observe the voices that serve us well.

In moments of solitude, we are gifted with the ability to connect deeply and authentically. When our minds are clear from clutter and distraction, we have a chance to truly hear both ourselves and others. It is in this connection that true miracles can manifest.

The Fast Track to True Genius

Japanese culture has a term *omoiyari*. It can be loosely described as someone's ability to understand, or to imagine, others' perspectives *and* selflessly serve them. Based on the root words *omoi*, or thought, and *yaru*, or give, the concept asks us to consider others' thoughts and actively support them. In Japanese tradition, the word isn't about feeling—it's about behavior. Because practicing omoiyari is meaningless if we do not adjust our own instincts and behaviors. It is impossible to do that if we cannot quiet the voices in our heads.

From time to time, I'll catch a glimmer of understanding in Uncle Barry's eyes, a deep desire to connect with me. It's human instinct to lower our barriers and find safe, common ground with those around us. That's why I'll never refuse a conversation with him. When I look at him, I can see how deeply he needs compassion—for someone to *see* him, without fear or judgment. So, I act on that need. I play along, responding to his Sam Cooke question over and over, no matter how many times he asks. The conversation isn't about me—it doesn't really matter whether I know who Sam Cooke is. The conversation is about serving him.

If we're distracted by voices in our head, we can't access that ability. We feel angry at others for not seeing us, so we demand their attention. Rather than using our conversations to serve others, we use them to serve ourselves, each party shouting into the fortress of the other's mind.

Inner silence—focus—is the foundation of emotional intelligence (EQ), a skill I use almost interchangeably with omoiyari. EQ is the ability to observe and manage self and others. Research studies have considered EQ a greater predictor of success than our intellect. In short, when you are conscious and connected, you will have a serious edge in all aspects of life. EQ is also connected to well-being and happiness. Conscious connections achieved through the four habits of LOVE (listen, observe, value, engage) are a powerful and simple way to increase emotional intelligence—fast! It starts with inner silence and reflection. When we bring inner silence into our conversations, we make space to consider how others feel. Imagining those emotions allows us to serve them. And serving others through listening makes *our* lives better—strengthening our self-perception, interpersonal skills, decision-making, self-expression, and stress management.

Emotional intelligence is a priceless skill that is worth the years it will take to master.

It requires us to bring consciousness into every conversation we have. We simply cannot connect with others unless we get quiet. Look at your interactions as an expression of your kindness and usefulness in the world. Share your mind's most valuable assets with the world. Today, tame your tongue and your thoughts.

Marcus needed to be more conscious about his intentions before his meeting. By going into the meeting focused on his own experiences, his own background, his own emotions, and his own goals and needs, he missed Keisha's many signals. He simply couldn't observe her fidgeting in her chair and glancing at the time. He also didn't notice the keychain hanging from her car keys revealing that she went to a school in his hometown. I noticed it right away. It never came up. It was a perfect opportunity to start with a shared experience. As a result, he couldn't get the support he needed. This was an EQ disaster. He was unable to see or manage himself and others.

Here Marcus's story illustrates a crucial point. We often assume a lack of emotional intelligence offends others—and very often it does. And yet his meeting was in *his* best interest. He walked away from a wonderful opportunity to gain access to key knowledge through a connection. Keisha, a leader who has learned to listen, sat patiently and listened to his rambling.

By failing to listen, he didn't harm anyone. But he might have lost about one million dollars. This is the amount another speaker made over three years after forging a connection with Keisha.

Whether we realize it or not, our ability to connect is the path to everything that we desire. At the heart of omoiyari is the concept of selfless service. When we prioritize what we are absorbing from the connections with others, we always gain something. When we listen to others to connect and train our emotional intelligence muscle, we access connection, greater intelligence, and miracles. Listening is a portal to wisdom.

Listen to Measure Success

When I want to gauge a meeting's success, I ask one simple question. I don't think about how smart I sounded. I don't count the *ums* and *ers* I used. I don't analyze the structure or focus of my delivery. I simply ask: *Did I listen more than I spoke?* If the answer is yes, I can almost guarantee the other person found the meeting successful.

That one question is the easiest, quickest shortcut to creating a strong connection. By consciously listening, you demonstrate the qualities that make great leaders—focus and empathy. When I was doing therapy before becoming a leadership strategist, I got to see how important it was for people to be heard. In corporate environments, I've been painfully aware of how touched leaders and professionals at all levels are to have someone who really listens without strings attached.

Humans have an inherent need to communicate. We want to listen and to be heard—and we value both sides of a conversation. When we share our ideas with the world, we give a part of ourselves. Being listened to makes us feel that gift is not in vain. No wonder listening is so valuable; it's a way of telling others they matter. The value of listening, in other words, is larger than any message—because the *act of listening* allows others to feel heard. By listening—a rare and valuable skill in our distracted, multitasking world—we not only demonstrate that a speaker's message is valuable. We also acknowledge the speaker's inherent value as a person who deserves to be heard.

We gain their wisdom and their respect. And when we don't listen—when we let the voices in our head drown out everything around us—we lose both.

That was obvious to anyone in the room with Marcus and Keisha—*except Marcus.* He overlooked the power of listening. While he could have gained enormous value from Keisha's insights, he focused on his impressive resume and brilliant ideas instead. He hounded me for a week to get him connected to her, yet forgot that the entire point of the connection was to listen. And he lost access to the real prize—the life-giving force of connection.

A Tale of Two Promotions

Ambitious, motivated, and hard-working, Sherry should have been her company's most valuable employee. She held a master's degree from Georgetown University, where she'd also co-developed a statewide initiative to support and mentor new entrepreneurs. Even with so much on her plate, she finished her graduate program at the top of her class and went on to work at a highly respected hospitality corporation.

She loved the job at first. Still, as the days, months, and years ticked by, she started to feel stuck. She told me about a colleague. "Derik and I started at the same time," she told me. "But he was promoted out of our office about—what?—two years ago."

I nodded, taking in her story.

"I tried to be happy for him . . ."

"Why weren't you?" I asked.

She looked at me, defeated. "I really thought I was next in line for that promotion," she admitted. As she leaned down to adjust something in her tote bag, I heard her take a deep breath. When she sat up again, her eyes were red. "I just figured . . . I tried to just tell myself I would be next."

"What's happened since then?" I asked.

She gave a little huff of a laugh. "It's not just Derik. They hired this new girl, Jenny. She is smart, but clearly less senior than most of the office. But, young, thin, blonde." She gave me a pointed look. "Talia, get this." Leaning across the table, she said, "She got promoted after only a year. And now she's higher than me!" She spat out the last phrase, angry and confused. After pausing for a moment, she spoke again, this time in a quiet voice of defeat. "What do you think? Is it because I'm a Black woman? I feel like Derik spent most of his time chatting and laughing with people. He always has this big smile on his face and doesn't seem stressed about deadlines. Jenny is always trying to lead us with eloquent speeches and games. I focus on my work and am the most productive. Is there anything I can do?"

Feeling her sense of powerlessness, I affirmed her perspective. "There could be many reasons, some in and out of your control," I said. "The good news is that there *is always* something you can do. You have power over your own approach."

She cocked her head to the side, but I could see the wheels turning behind her eyes. Finally, she replied, "Okay."

"So, for the next 90 days, I want you to practice one thing." I didn't tell her to focus on her work, take initiative, get organized, or any other good suggestion to improve her chances of getting a promotion. I told her to study and improve how she listens. To guide the exercise, I gave her a list of things to listen for. I suggested she listen for statements that reflect a speaker's values. Things like, "We need more *data*," "I hope the *team* can really *step it up*," or "We need to focus on *morale*." Beyond just language, I urged her to listen for tone, the hidden messages in jokes or sarcasm, and the topics that made a team or group go silent. I also gave her questions to replace small talk around the office:

What is important to you these days?

What energizes you?

What value do you bring to the team?

What kinds of things excite you in general?

What are your top two priorities?

She left the conversation skeptical about my advice, but for the next three months, she did as I suggested. When we met again, everything had changed. She was invited to additional, high-profile meetings, even receiving an award at one of the team events. A few months later, Sherry finally got that promotion. She had a complete transformation. After years of banging her head against the wall, one challenge and one consistent habit changed her life.

"This is amazing," she gushed. "It's like a miracle." I'm happy for Sherry, and she's right. It feels like a miracle, and it's something that's available to all of us. It's the power of a simple, yet life-changing habit. And you can learn to do it every day.

Tearing Down the Fortress

Like Sherry, many will be skeptical or think it is a stretch to think that a simple habit like listening can change your life. I have found that most miracles or astonishing results start with simple changes. The barrier to making substantial changes in your listening is something called "overconfidence bias." When you think you've "got this" or you are overconfident that certain things just don't matter, you cut yourself off from critical wisdom. I can recall so many times in my life when I really believed that I knew what was best. When I struggled in business early on, there was a part of me that felt like I was doomed. Instead of listening to that voice, I went on a listening tour, collecting different perspectives and ways of seeing things. Listening to different perspectives was my first step toward mastering this skill. It will lead you to better results, reduced stress, and enhanced clarity. How many courses have you taken on mastering the art of listening? According to recent studies, individuals with strong listening skills tend to have more successful careers and healthier relationships than those who struggle with listening. Yet we do not create opportunities to train ourselves because it feels so natural and simple. Steve Jobs, former CEO of Apple, famously said, "Simple can be harder than complex: You have to work hard to get your thinking clean to make it simple. But it's worth it in the end because once you get there, you can move mountains."[3] Conscious listening is about cleaning your thinking and simplifying your intentions.

There are so many benefits of strong listening skills. The more you listen to others and tune out distractions, the simpler things become, and the easier it is to achieve mutual goals. In one study, individuals who listened actively showed a significant increase in productivity and reduced anxiety levels.[4] In another study, couples who actively listened to each other during arguments had a higher chance of staying together long term.[5]

What if improving this one skill was the real answer to most of your problems? Poor listening skills can have detrimental effects on your mental health and success. Without listening, we miss out on opportunities, leave important questions unanswered, and move away from opportunities to exchange value. Misunderstandings and missed opportunities can lead to stress, anxiety, low self-esteem, and strained relationships.

My uncle Barry has a kind heart. Before his illness stole him from our family, he got along with everybody. His easygoing attitude drew people to him like a magnet, and most people connected deeply with his energy.

Marcus brought a similar enthusiasm to his meeting with Keisha. Thoroughly prepared—and very excited—he set out to prove his value to her by rattling off his accomplishments. He spoke clearly with very few *ums* and *ers*, even as he charged through his resume, but the conversation was completely unbalanced.

Executives who multitask in front of others, parents who worry more about their kids' success than their kids' well-being, and employees who internalize every criticism all share the inability to listen. They are addicted to a tape on repeat in their heads. They all have their own fixation, their own version of Sam Cooke. Like the research participants forced to say a single, meaningless word repeatedly, they're trapped inside the fortresses of their minds. The harder they try to communicate, the louder the voices grow. The louder the voices grow, the more impenetrable the fortress. It's a spiral that can only lead to isolation, dissatisfaction, and anger.

If we want to tear down the walls around our minds, we must implement true conscious listening. Listening consciously is so transformative, it will feel like a magic bullet. To connect, learn, and access miracles, a few concrete steps are needed to improve both your listening and your emotional intelligence. First, we must pay attention to the ways we typically listen. Everyone brings different habits to the table, but I find that people typically fall into one of five listening styles. Our listening habits can also reveal underlying wants and needs.

1. **Thrill seeker:** You are drawn to exciting messages; you tune out when a speaker isn't entertaining. You are drawn to dynamic speakers. You want to escape boredom.

2. **Ranker:** You often disregard messages from people of a lower social status. You stop everything for those in high positions. You want approval and security.

3. **Fact hunter:** You scan messages for facts, statistics, and figures. Emotional content and abstract ideas rarely draw your attention. You tend to evaluate the validity of the message and potentially miss important context. You want validation and to feel superior.

4. **Plugger:** You listen primarily for opportunities to connect the speaker's message to your own personal experience. You try to find a way to "plug" your value before assessing if it is relevant to the speaker's intentions or needs. You want to control.

5. **Helper:** You interject advice and listen for problem-solving opportunities even when the person you're listening to simply needs to be heard. You want validation.

All these listening types share a common flaw—they listen for the opportunity to meet their own needs. Some needs are superficial and harmless, like wanting a chance to share an exciting idea. Others have a deep need to feel important and struggle with the fear of being forgotten. The best way to fix this is to do work on self-esteem. We can build self-esteem by doing estimable acts. Listening is an estimable act that I try to do as often as possible. Good listeners are often more self-confident. They have a great sense of self. They do the work to feel good about who they are, and they don't look for love in all the wrong places. Instead, they see themselves as having a lot to give, and they consider their time and attention as assets that they are open to sharing with the world.

Conscious listening is about serving others. If we want to build deeper, stronger, more successful connections, we have to bring some skill—like our emotional intelligence—to the table. That means practicing omoiyari—setting ourselves aside and giving the gift of still, real listening.

Once we become aware of our listening habits, we can adjust—when we enter conversations with another person, instead of relying on our old, ineffective habits, we can come into the conversation with a conscious, thoughtful purpose.

The purpose may be to connect. Or it might be to teach. Maybe it's to learn something by asking questions. Or to inspire, motivate, comfort, or simply be present.

I aim to begin every conversation by consciously choosing my purpose. And if I don't have a purpose, I don't open my mouth.

Listening requires us to be conscious, to build our relationships not just out of habit but out of choice. It requires us to focus. And when we genuinely focus, we naturally signal our interest. We ask questions, clarify details, recap main points, and build a sense of connection with everyone we encounter. That's what it takes to be a leader. It's not easy but it's worth it.

Through listening, we can wake up. We can transform ourselves from mediocre zombies to thriving, happy, connected human beings.

Imagine approaching a difficult team member and just listening to their point of view. Imagine putting down your phone and listening to the conversations happening around you. Imagine dropping your pen, your notebook, and your checklists, then going outside and listening to the wisdom of a chirping bird. How many voices go unnoticed and unheard? What if you quieted your thoughts and invited those voices into true, purposeful conversation? What could you discover? What could you learn? How could you change? Who could you become?

A Miracle

Most people don't know what would happen if they truly listened because they've never really done it. For as long as they can remember, they've focused on their own needs, demanding that others listen—but refusing to listen themselves.

When I gave Sherry that assignment, she didn't know what would happen. Even though she felt she was being ignored, I wanted her to work on listening to others. For 90 days, she focused on how she was listening. And it changed her life.

When we met again, I asked her what she'd learned from the experience. She told me she hadn't even realized how strained her listening had been. She also reflected on her relationship with Derik, who was promoted two years ahead of her. If she had to describe him in a nutshell, she would say that he was a great listener and always asked great questions. "Why do you think that is?" he would say. "I wonder if there is an easy fix to that problem" was a common response. "How can I support you?" he'd ask daily. She realized that Derik knew so much about her—her complaints, her quirks, who she liked and didn't like in the office. He was always so engaged with people. Yet she knew very little about him.

Sherry had a painful epiphany: She never really asked him any questions. She had a very different style. During meetings, she often focused on herself, constantly questioning how others felt about her. A constant loop played in her mind: *What are they thinking of me? What should I do? He's being rude. Why are their faces blank? Nobody cares what I think.*

Then she started listening. By quieting the voices in her head, she allowed the room's shared messages to resonate. And she started to connect. She linked together ideas that seemed separate before, strengthened bonds with longtime coworkers, and learned more about her organization. Once she tuned in to her listening habits, she immediately realized what she was doing wrong. She was sabotaging herself by failing to connect with others. She plugged her ears with resentment and self-centered fear. Her world was about survival with no path or vision for what it feels like to thrive as a community, culture, or team. When she listened and finally brought omoiyari to her work, she recognized others. And, in turn, others recognized her. By listening, she was finally heard.

Her new awareness eventually became second nature. In the end, she told me, it was just like any other habit. She couldn't imagine going back to the endless negative self-talk—the distracting, destructive chatter in her head. After just a few months, she no longer had to think about how to listen. It became part of her.

Moments of listening are moments of presence—opportunities to give a rare gift. By breathing deeply and refusing to judge, we remind ourselves of the joy of connection. We free ourselves of the need to solve every problem, evaluate every statement, complete every task, and entertain ourselves at every turn.

In exchange for truly listening, we gain intense compassion for others and the ability to connect with people for who they are—not who we expect them to be. It's an illuminating experience!

Sherry struggled to be heard until she learned how to listen. She had the power to change her situation all along. We all do. By increasing her listening awareness, she gained a level of understanding that helped her navigate her company and eventually leave her job to become a very successful entrepreneur.

If I were granted one wish for the world, it would be that people listen to one another. Nothing is more fulfilling than listening to understand, without judgment or agenda. The richest form of connection, conscious listening acknowledges the inherent value of our stories, experiences, values, celebrations, and pain.

Listen to Master the Art of the Shift

The most powerful way that I have used the LOVE system to help leaders is during an activity that I do both in leadership development classes and on large stages. I call it "The Art of the Shift," and it's my signature event.

As a leadership strategist, I have found that shedding a clear light on the inner voices and introducing a new thought pattern is a highly effective method to facilitate rapid transformation in leaders. Whether I'm in a classroom or on a large stage, this exercise helps individuals increase emotional intelligence using thoughts and feelings to get unstuck.

Here is how it works: I invite a volunteer on stage to share work or life challenges. They sit facing the audience, while I stand behind them and listen intently. The volunteer shares one challenge. It can be on any topic—everything from weight loss struggles to fears about society and the world.

After they briefly share their challenge, I ask them to share their three most deeply held values. Then, without preparation or hesitation, I create a stream of thoughts more aligned with their core values. I become the voice in their head, speaking as if I am them. It's like in the movie *Freaky*

Friday, where the mother and daughter switch bodies and live each other's lives.

It's important for me to listen carefully and observe their body language so that I can reframe their entire situation in a way that gives them an instant feeling of relief. This exercise requires me to listen with a level of mastery, taking notes and fully immersing myself in the moment.

By listening for underlying needs and desires, I can provide a new perspective that aligns with their core values. I pay attention to their mood, tone, and nonverbal cues. It's a powerful moment that not only affects the participant on stage but also the entire audience.

Through this exercise, individuals gain greater self-awareness and improve their ability to think clearly about what to do next. They are no longer stuck. It's a reminder that true connection requires us to be present, to listen deeply, and to be open to reframing our thoughts and perspectives. When we do this, we can create the conditions that lead to innovative ideas and meaningful plans.

In this book, the "Art of the Shift" will be an easy-to-access, no-cost tool to master LOVE and remain conscious and connected to your goals and values.

I stood on the stage looking out at the mass of theater seating, surrounded by hundreds of others—if not a thousand—in the audience laser focused on this spontaneous exercise I do on stage to improve emotional intelligence. Snaking down one of the auditorium's aisles, 150 people stood in a line that ended beyond the door, through the old-fashioned, burgundy-draped lobby, and out into the cool, foggy Detroit night. All waiting for the opportunity to come on stage for a shift in perspective that feels more like a shot of relief that boosts energy and motivation. The line shifted forward, and a 40-something man walked toward me.

"Hi!" I said. "What's your name?"

My words disappeared into this man, an energy void personified. Shoulders sloped; his rumpled suit seemed to hang on his shoulders. Tufts of hair stuck out slightly over the tops of his ears. As he approached, he didn't even smile. This man was the very picture of busy, stressed, and disengaged.

He grunted a greeting in reply and looked at me sheepishly. "I'm Cole," he replied.

Smiling warmly and holding eye contact, I asked, "What challenge are you facing?"

He knew the question was coming. I asked it of every person who had joined me on that stage so far, and I would ask it of many more before the evening was over. I'd been cycling through a line of volunteers. One participant would sit down as two more would join the line, creating an endless demand for this one simple exercise. As each new volunteer approached me on stage, I asked for two things: their problem and their values. Then I used the values to help people gain clarity about the truth and feelings behind the issue.

Brave but tired, this man had joined about a third of the way through the event and, as he trudged up the stairs, I had an inkling of what he was about to say.

"My boss gives terrible feedback," he said, clearing his throat.

I let silence hang in the air for a moment, sensing he had more to say. I was right.

"Every time I ask for feedback—and we're supposed to ask for feedback every quarter—but every time I ask, he says the rudest things. Then I just feel like . . . well . . ."

I smiled and raised my eyebrows.

"I just feel bad for the rest of the day. I don't know how much longer I can do it. I feel completely drained, numb, and starting to really resent this guy," he sighed.

Conflicts with leadership or those in power are some of the most common issues I hear about from people at all career levels and places in their lives. It comes up everywhere, not only at events like "The Art of the Shift," but also in retreat and training classrooms. Day after day, people tell me about their workplace woes, and while they may not use words like alienated, disconnected, or disengaged, the sense of feeling cut off from everything and everyone around them is palpable.

Even though I'd heard the challenge of being drained and frustrated with a boss a million times before, I was just as excited as ever to help Cole address it. Because people who feel disconnected, like lost, cut-off zombies, are the people I can help most.

I affirmed his concern, but moved quickly into the *real* question: "What are your values?"

He'd been waiting alongside the stage for some time watching others go through the exercise, so he knew what I was about to ask. "Family, integrity, and joy," he declared, the most confident thing I'd heard him say the entire time, including the greeting.

"Ah, okay," I replied. "Face forward." I gently guided his shoulder until he took a few steps forward. Then I stepped behind him. Feet shifting and neck rolling, I could tell he was uncomfortable. I hoped not for long.

"My boss is such a jerk," I whined, taking on Cole's persona by adopting his vocal demeanor. I added a little huff at the end for effect. I heard a few snickers from the audience, but as had been the case the entire night, you could hear a pin drop. I continued the shift.

"One thing's for sure," I continued. *"I'm in this job because I love how it allows me to support my family. I also have a lot of integrity, and I have chosen to show up to this job and do my best. I'm clear that some people are happy here, and some people have quirks. I'm okay today because I'm choosing to be joyful. Joy is my common theme, and just because someone else is not a part of my joy, I don't have to align with that misery. I'm liking my life these days."*

At that point, I saw his posture shift. The change was barely noticeable, but it was there if you were looking for it—and I was definitely looking. The purpose of the shift is to physically see a bit of relief.

I went on, *"I love the choices I'm making to spend time with my family. I love how I'm honest. I love that I am in control. When my boss goes off, I can sit there, smile, and manage my own behavior. I like it when I choose to have integrity as a professional, no matter what I see other people doing in the world. I'm good. I'm feeling great today. I wonder what else I can do to feel happier and joyful. I bet I can plan a family vacation."*

I paused for a moment to signal the end of the exercise. When I stepped behind him, his eyes were dark and saggy, and I could see that he was chewing on the inside of his cheek. He looked destitute, like a stock trader on Black Tuesday. Now he spun around to face me. He looked like he had a facelift. "Oh, my goodness, what just happened?! I feel so good!" he said, suspicious of this sudden shift. I thought he might hug me, but he realized that we just met, so instead he turned and made his way off the stage.

As he made his way back to his seat, I heard him murmur, "That was magical."

Cole is one of the few that I checked on after the shift on a big stage. I could see that he was really struggling. During the shift, I only allow people to give me a slice of the details because that is all I need. However, I am aware that humans have complex lives and there are often multiple things contributing to how someone feels in the moment. So, what happened after Cole listened to a value-based version of his life? Well, first, the drama with his boss became less of a priority. He was able to shift his attention to other activities. He devoted himself to writing the novel he had been wanting to write for so long and blossomed into an exemplary leader within his team. More importantly, with a lighter emotional life, he started exercising, traveling more, and shared that he was just downright happier.

Your state of being is connected to your ability to stay on the path. Listen to how you frame things and reach for relief and an improved feeling. That could be enough to unlock your power. An enhanced mood is a sign of progress. It's not only rewarding, but it connects you to the journey that lies ahead and aids in unlocking your power. Listen closely to the words you use to describe situations. Aim for thoughts that support your well-being. This could be all that you need to liberate yourself from any limitations!

The art of the shift is one of the most powerful action steps you can take. Doing this shifting exercise is the fast track to instantly practicing the LOVE system for transformation. It requires you to listen to yourself, observe the world around you, consider your values, and engage in communication that supports a fresh perspective.

When we think about conscious connections, we often imagine connection to others and the outside world. *Yes!* This is a critical part of a rich life. However, you can only successfully lead others, creating a life you love and accomplishing great things, if you master your connection with yourself. The shift is a very practical way to practice self-love. When you listen to your inner guidance, observe your habits, honor your values, and connect within, you build a power so strong that it effortlessly radiates warmth and light to everyone.

Mastering the art of the shift can give you access to instant relief that, practiced over time, will energize you to achieve your goals and dreams and help others do the same.

Do You Believe in Magic?

When I talked to Cole at that "The Art of the Shift" event in Detroit, I had never met him before. The same is true of the dozens of other people who joined me on stage that night. Over the years, I've done that exercise with hundreds of people, and most are shocked at the transformation they feel. Sometimes they want to replicate it in themselves.

As I tell them, it just takes focus and connection.

The art of the shift requires us to apply the wisdom we gain when we listen, observe, and value every single day. And, when it's time to listen, we use this wisdom to reframe our lives. We create magic in ourselves and others.

While Cole's transformation was memorable, it wasn't an anomaly. The "Art of the Shift" experience fascinates and inspires people every time it happens. Often, people describe this experience just as Cole did that night: magic.

The LOVE system *is magic*. It gives us the power to transform. It helps us wake up and take control of the nightmare we are creating in our minds. You can engage your mind to help you solve challenges. You can engage others to inspire change. Engaging is the application of listening, observing, and realigning with our values.

As I've taken this exercise around the country, I've worked with people in all areas of their lives. Sometimes—perhaps most often—people complain about work. Other times, I hear things like, "My kid keeps getting in fights at school," or "My neighbors party every weekend night and we can't get any sleep," or "I hate the state of our society today." Every time, I give them a quick shift, and they go on their way, murmuring one thing over and over: *magic*.

That magic is a skill—and if you've been following along in this book so far, you're ready to try it.

The world is ready, too.

Listen to Drive Change

Not long ago, I received a message from a man who was raised by an unapologetically racist father. With beliefs that fundamentally opposed his own, his dad openly expressed what he called "disturbing hate" for other races. Concerned about raising his kids around racist beliefs, he decided to cut ties with him.

After sharing a long list of details about his father's beliefs, Chris asked me for advice. I was touched by the request because I didn't know him well. His story was challenging—many listeners would have been distracted, sorting through their own pain and anger as they reacted to the father's comments. As a Black woman, I could have easily defaulted to my own opinions about his father. I could have been sucked into a dramatic response that had little to do with my commitment to LOVE. However, this conversation wasn't about me. It wasn't about a cause. It wasn't even about racism, necessarily. The conversation was about Chris's difficult decision to cut ties with his father.

No matter the reason, disconnecting from family is a hard and painful decision. He'd taken a hard step to preserve his own values. And, more than anything, he needed the gift of a conscious connection.

I didn't have a solution—and it didn't matter. That wasn't what he needed.

So, I offered him a listening ear. Without absorbing his pain or using his struggle to validate my own worldview, I joined a purposeful conversation. I chose to show compassion.

To give that gift, I had to listen—I needed to imagine that he was the only person in the room, processing his message through a lens of what he needed at that moment. The conversation demanded emotional intelligence. It demanded omoiyari.

We do not have to be afraid of differences. We can connect with people, even when challenges seem difficult to overcome. We accomplish this by practicing listening to appreciate, not evaluate.

We can bring a thoughtful, open mind to our tasks, despite what's happening around us. And we can make the world a better, brighter, safer place. If we want to achieve all that, we must go beyond hearing—we must make a habit of really listening, immersing ourselves in the spirit of omoiyari.

With purposeful curiosity and vulnerability, we must aim to discover who people are and what unique values they bring to the world. This is hardest, of course, when their messages differ from our own perspective. If we can remain undisturbed, fascinated, and open as others share their differing viewpoints, we reap the rewards of conscious connections.

I wasn't born with the ability to give that gift. Over the years, I've practiced my listening skills until I was prepared to hear stories like Chris's. You can do the same.

The Case for Greatness

In his autobiography, Nelson Mandela reflects on his interactions with local, regional, national, and international leaders. Mandela is known for his stirring brilliance—his ability to condense leadership lessons into pithy, elegant provocations that stick in listeners' minds long after the lesson is taught.

When Mandela had the opportunity to interact with the great leaders of his time, he didn't focus on speaking. Instead, he watched and listened, learning as he did how tribal leaders, presidents, and diplomats approached conflict. As they settled disputes and tried cases, he observed. They told stories, and he listened.

For years he practiced this strategy, finally settling on a profound truth. *The most powerful leaders spent little time speaking.* Instead, they listened and observed. They honored their values. And they showed up, every day, to engage the people who trusted them to lead.

That's the foundation of the LOVE system.

What separates us from Mandela? What divides us from history's changemakers? What made Martin Luther King Jr. and Mother Teresa so memorable?

We are currently living in a time of radical transformation, known as the Fourth Industrial Revolution. Technology has dramatically changed our lives and is continuing to do so at an exponential rate. The Industrial Revolution offers us both opportunities and dilemmas that must be explored if we want to understand why and how humanity thrives. Klaus Schwab, chairman and founder of the World Economic Forum and author of *The Fourth Industrial Revolution,* highlighted how artificial intelligence (AI) has revolutionized our ever evolving world. He concluded that to make truly significant advances, we must come together as one, leveraging all sources of wisdom such as mental strength, empathy, and spirituality. How do we stay ahead in an ever-changing world and make a meaningful impact? To "mobilize our minds, hearts, and souls," the first steps are to listen attentively, observe closely, clarify our values, and engage actively.[6] This will help us remain conscious of what's happening around us while connecting with others as great leaders have done throughout history— inspiring how we lead and influencing what we stand for.

The foundation for greatness is rooted in the ability to master LOVE. Our capacity to approach listening as an art form strengthens our effectiveness to use LOVE and develop it over a lifetime.

The Greatest Edge

Listening is a fundamental skill that supports all other skills. We listen to others not only to gain wisdom but also as a way of giving back. While the self-serving benefits are evident, listening is the foundation for building relationships, nurturing new ideas, and honing our intelligence. Through attentive ears we can better understand ourselves and those around us as well as uncover life's deeper mysteries. Listening invites us into an expansive space that enables us to discern what truly matters in this world.

To make informed decisions, it is essential that we learn how to listen—not just to our external environment but also within ourselves, tuning in to an inner dialogue that will both inspire us and give us the courage we need.

Moments of listening are moments of presence—they are opportunities to give a rare gift. By breathing deeply and refusing to judge, I remind myself of the joy of connection. I free myself of the need to solve every problem, evaluate every statement, complete every task, and entertain myself at every turn.

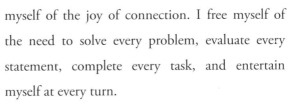

Shifting your attitude from one of rushed anticipation for the future to an open-minded attentiveness opens you up to the rewards of listening.

In exchange for truly listening, I've gained an intense compassion for others and the ability to connect with people for the purpose of learning, growing, or even being entertained. Shifting your attitude from one of rushed anticipation for the future to an open-minded attentiveness opens you up to the rewards of listening. The act of listening forces you to pause and take pleasure in being connected with others. And, if you need a little nugget for the ego, if you start practicing this consistently, you will, without a doubt, quickly become one of the smartest people in the room. It is the greatest edge in the modern age of digital distraction. It might also make you rich. The rewards are exhilarating!

Listening is a learned skill or an intention to be present in the moment. Listening is about consciously slowing your thoughts down, pausing your perspectives, managing your emotions, and appreciating the experience that listening provides. It requires you to meditate and reflect on an experience with another person or group of people. In its purest form, you may not have to do anything with what you hear. Train your mind to listen with a clean slate. Once you have reached this state, you then can take in others' ideas and internalize them. You can activate empathy to experience life in someone else's life movie. Do you interrupt or talk back to movie screens? Most of us don't. We are there to appreciate the characters and the scripts.

Listening doesn't require agreement, but it demands presence.

Listening doesn't require agreement, but it demands presence.

TAKEAWAYS

In this chapter, we've learned the importance of listening as an act of compassion beyond that of simple hearing. Listening is a learned skill or an intention. Listening is about being present in the moment. Listening is about consciously slowing your thoughts down, pausing your perspectives, managing your emotions, and appreciating the experience that listening provides.

Listening builds emotional intelligence.
Listening improves mental health.

Below are key ideas to take with you:

- **Establish purpose.** To foster an effective meeting or conversation, we need to establish what it is that both parties want from the interaction. Do they need advice? A kind ear? Support? Are you looking to learn something? To teach? Whatever it is, we should adjust our listening habit accordingly before the interaction begins.

- **Quiet your mind.** To listen, we must quiet the unnecessary worries and distractions in our minds. It is vital to listen with the intent to understand rather than to respond. We must clear our thoughts to open that space for deeper consideration and, therefore, connection.

- **Practice omoiyari.** The act of listening is a precious gift. For people to feel heard, we have to suspend our own selfish desires and instead place the focus on our conversational partner and their needs. Listen as a service to others to build deeper connections and improve our interactions.

- **Did I listen more than I spoke?** After a conversation, it's helpful to reflect on your communication skills. You can start by assessing your listening skills and identifying areas for improvement. Next, reflect on your emotions during the conversation. Were you able to stay present and engaged, or did distractions and emotions interfere? Finally, evaluate the extent to which you engaged in active listening during the conversation, and use how much you learned about the other person as one measure of success.

- **Listen to the voices in your head.** Shift by questioning the stories you tell yourself about your life. Are they true? Do they align with your values and goals? If not, it's time to reframe them.

- **Take the 90-day listening challenge.** Ask people these questions in your own words and listen:

  - What is important to you these days?

  - What energizes you?

  - What value do you bring to the team?

  - What kinds of things excite you in general?

  - What are your top two priorities?

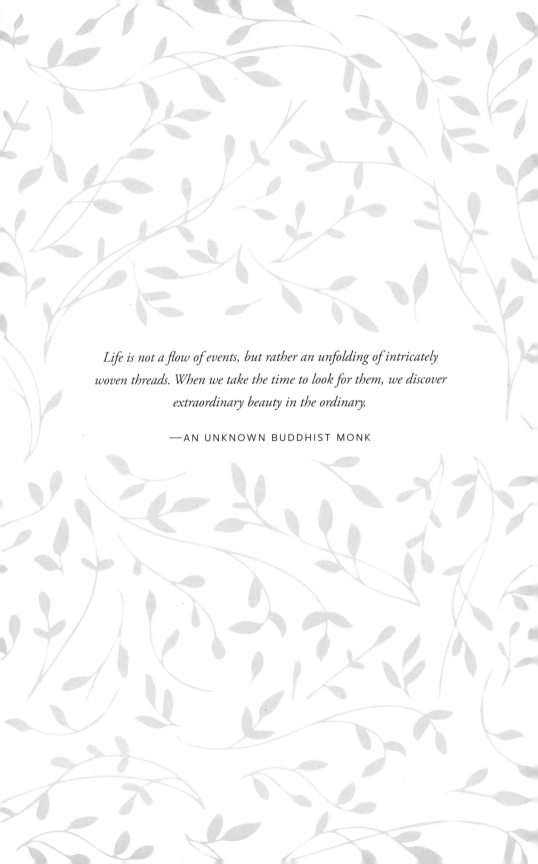

Life is not a flow of events, but rather an unfolding of intricately woven threads. When we take the time to look for them, we discover extraordinary beauty in the ordinary.

—AN UNKNOWN BUDDHIST MONK

CHAPTER THREE

OBSERVE

———

Pay Attention and Watch My Signal

The converted garage was cramped with instruments and equipment—drums, guitars, keyboards, amps, and microphones everywhere. It was my dad's rehearsal space for his band. As a young girl, I watched in awe as they practiced together, each musician weaving their instruments into a cohesive sound.

I studied my father, the drummer in the band, as he directed and kept the rhythm, communicating with his bandmates through subtle nods and gestures. I observed how they played together, seamlessly blending sounds and notes into a symphony of music. This is where I learned the art of observation.

My father would always find ways to include me and my brother, Joey, in the rehearsals without disrupting the flow. Even though we had limited musical abilities, he would still give us tasks like using drumsticks to act like the band director or signaling the lead singer when it was time for me to help sing the bridge of the song. He encouraged us to listen and observe carefully, to notice how different sounds came together and to feel the emotions each song conveyed.

"Pay attention and watch my signal," my father whispered as he raised his eyebrows just enough to let me know that I needed to decide. I could go high or go low with my voice. The choice was mine. My father trained me to sing with the band and anticipate the drumbeat and the notes. He taught me to read the room—to determine when and how I would use my voice.

In the literal sense, at rehearsal, I followed the band's signals to determine what to do next. When you become a lead singer, you give the signal, and the band follows you. This lesson applies to the journey to a more conscious and connected (purposeful) life. It requires you to listen to different voices and views, observe signals that guide your next move, develop yourself, and build interdependent relationships with people you respect. Then, you step into the spotlight and lead without ever forgetting how to follow. In rehearsal, there was a magical combination of listening to great music, watching each band member play individually and together, and taking moments to deviate from the plan to feel the music and go with the flow.

The brown shag carpet was flattened from my usual spot next to my dad's drum set. We sat there, cross-legged, in the corner of our living room, listening to the live band play five or six songs already. My thrift store Care Bear pajamas were just as worn as the carpet beneath us.

With a shake of his head and a little puff of a chuckle, my father gingerly lifted his drumsticks, making a dramatic start. "Uh one, two. Uh one, two, three, four," the band erupted into sound, my cousin Kevin on the keyboard, Mark on the bass, and my dad leading it all. This rehearsal day was all about Bob Marley hits.

As the song ended, he rested the sticks on his lap as he casually rattled off Marley's personal history. Born on his grandmother's farm in Nine Mile, Jamaica, the reggae legend quickly realized his ability to truly *see* those around him. He began reading palms at just four years old, and those around him took note of his uncanny ability to predict others' future— perhaps through clairvoyance, but just as possibly through his ability to connect with others, the very thing that made his music so powerful. By the time he turned seven— about the age I was when I sat next to my dad during band rehearsal—he'd decided to become a singer.

My dad rattled off these facts with the ease of a seasoned music professor. Barely able to read, he didn't learn this stuff in school. He simply heard it. After years of playing on pots and pans, and finding his passion in music, he came to know these legends' stories as well as he knew his own.

"We'll play one more. A live one, but let's listen to it first," he said, selecting a sleeve bordered in the bold colors of the Jamaican flag. Expertly, he dropped the needle at the record's outer edge. The eager anticipation of a crowd poured from the speaker, followed by a man's voice promising "a Trenchtown experience." Almost imperceptibly, the audience's cheers morphed into the easy rhythm of the drums, and the soaring guitar, somehow both tinny and rich. Dad's band didn't join in; we all just stopped to listen.

As though the opening drum riff was connected to my dad by an invisible string, my dad started to sway, just slightly, and his eyes fell closed. I usually closed my eyes when he did. In hopes of capturing just a drop of the bliss that came over him when he listened to his albums, I mimicked his motions.

Sometimes, that night included, I just watched him. The music seemed to flow through his entire body, his movements effortless. Natural. His brow furrowed, then, and his eyes opened. As though we were the only two people on earth, he whispered, "Listen to this next part."

I furrowed my brow, too, recreating the look of studying for an important exam—the look that washed over my father's face when a remarkable passage played. At first, the rhythms continued unabated. Marley crooned, "One good thing about music," but as he reached the finale, the crowd's energy grew. It was responding to something on stage, their love of Marley, or just something in the air that night.

My father's lips parted, and with his eyes still closed, he murmured along with Marley: "When it hits, you feel no pain."

The record was well-loved, its sleeve worn white around the edges from the dozens of times my dad—and, I'm sure, whoever owned it before him—had pulled it out of his collection. Etched into the vinyl was the culture of dozens of island musicians, translated through Bob Marley's easy voice. And this poured into my father's ears. I strained to hear what my dad heard in those simple melodies and easy beats.

More than just songs, those records had stories to tell. The music burst to life through my father, more exciting than any Disney movie or PBS kids' show. Beyond notes, those melodies offered the most vivid images of worlds long ago lost to change, good and bad.

Each movement of the vocal cords and strum of the guitar was a choice—a code my father had cracked long ago. No matter how insignificant one beat seemed, it made sense with the next. That riff added to the next whiff of melody; you almost forgot that the record wasn't featuring a single player but a band of highly skilled musicians. The talented group was working together with their crowd, each sound balancing another and each rhythm driving the melody forward.

It was hard to understand at first. To really appreciate the *greats*, we had to listen. We had to strain to make sense of what was happening on the record—and what had inspired it. Trained musicians, like the ones who studied Bob Marley, could pick the music from a page. Noses pressed close to the chart, they could play each note and observe each rest, perfectly translating the notes to sounds.

That's not what the *greats* did. Like my dad, they just knew the music in their bones. They knew how to turn sound into a connection. They heard music everywhere, listening from the parishes to the beaches. Like gods collecting the gifts that were poured out all around them, they sifted through every tiny moment and molded it into a vinyl disc that transcended time.

My dad understood that intuitively. But he had to work for it. And so did I.

To really appreciate the *greats*, we had to listen. We had to strain to make sense of what was happening on the record—and what had inspired it.

They knew how to turn sound into a connection.

Observe Your Way to Mastery

Perhaps counterintuitively, the story of my dad's musical genius isn't about listening. Not really. It's about the power of taking in everything around us. It's about zooming out—beyond speaker and listener, beyond meetings, beyond work, and even family. It's about being *conscious*—alive—in the world. To observe is to be alive in the world.

My father played professionally worldwide without ever learning to read music. He'd mastered listening and observation. Then he auditioned for Frank Sinatra.

To observe is to be alive in the world.

Despite playing with passion and with all his soul, my father was told that they could not use him because he does not read music.

Without attending a fancy music school, he found a way for his brain to download his own Masterclass in calypso, jazz, rhythm and blues. He picked up everything he needed to know about the great players of our time—and then some.

Every drop of knowledge and wisdom was free. He replaced his lack of technical skills with an exaggerated genius and skill in both listening and observing.

He rose to levels of mastery in playing the drums by observing.

Listening is like that audition in many ways. Yes there are inherently good listeners, people who can engage with a speaker more naturally than others. But, like music, no matter how much natural talent you have, listening requires patience and observation. You must hear the music and read the notes to achieve mastery.

My father was innovative; he observed something else to compensate for his inability to read music. Beyond just listening, he hung around in nightclubs and music venues. When he wasn't playing a gig, he was connecting. He introduced himself to managers, workers, and fans, asking questions and hearing their stories. If he noticed a packed house, he homed in on those artists, memorizing their names and finding a way to hang around a bit more, picking up the records of the *greats* to feel their worn edges and smooth fronts.

He wasn't defensive or afraid to ask questions. He just watched and learned. And after a time spent tuning his ear to distinctions in sound, he didn't have to ask anymore. He heard the double strum of a funk riff and recognized Sister Sledge. When he heard easy, breathy falsetto, he pictured Earth, Wind & Fire.

He listened and observed for years. Straining to hear the combinations of players, instruments, styles, and periods, he picked up everything he could.

The skill of observation can instantly move you toward levels of mastery in your work and life. Like my dad did with his music, and like I've seen dozens of clients do with their talents, family, and community goals, this one skill can hand you the reins of your life. You'll achieve things you've never done before. Without changing anything but a habit, you will access 80 percent of the world you have been letting pass you by.

And this, my friends, is a critical step in creating a more conscious and connected world.

Earn Your Attention

John felt overlooked and insignificant. I could see it as clearly as if it were written across his face. Although I'm sure he thought he was hiding his feelings, his face fell a little more every time he spoke.

"I'm just asking," he said, "are there ways we could give ourselves more time for—"

"This isn't a time issue," Joseph interjected. "It's an issue of productivity rates."

Like clockwork, every head turned to Joseph, eyes fixed on him, even as he offered the team no practical solutions. I'd been anticipating the head turn. I'd carefully observed the meeting space for the past several weeks. Joseph tended to speak louder than John. At first, I assumed that was the reason people paid more attention to him. And I don't just mean a little more attention. I mean the type of attention that involves leaning in, nodding, and grunting little sounds of approval. The type of attention that means you get your way. The type of attention that means people really, truly trust you.

As I watched, week after week, I realized that it wasn't simply the volume of Joseph's voice. Sarah got the same type of attention, and her voice wasn't loud or booming.

"Would our productivity increase if we had more cutting-edge workspaces?" Sarah chimed in. The faces around the table turned immediately to her.

John's eyes widened, and he shook his head just slightly. The week before, he'd suggested revamping the faculty office space. Everybody had ignored him.

I'd been waiting for the moment to test my hypothesis. Just an intern, I wasn't expected to do much—but I'd been invited to jump in if I had thoughts. I had some thoughts, but they weren't related to the meeting's topic. My thoughts, at the time, were about the power of observation.

"I have some ideas for improving the productivity rate and outcomes," I said. Just as I suspected, all eyes flashed to me. "John's suggestion seems strong to me. Hiring more research assistants could give faculty more time, which would greatly impact how productive everyone is." I'd made the same suggestion as John. Where his words were dismissed, mine received the same thoughtful, enthusiastic head nods as Joseph and Sarah.

I made the same arguments others were making. So why were my ideas received with enthusiasm?

The secret to success could be hidden in a simple detail: they like the words "productivity rates"!

Observation is powerful. By paying attention to subtle reactions and analyzing how people respond to different words, behaviors, and choices, you can gain valuable insights into what motivates people—and unlock your potential for success.

Think of observation as listening to a beautiful song—each note tells a story, evoking an emotion. When you observe social situations, you can make conscious connections that will maximize your capacity to succeed, connect, and make a difference.

But mastering the art of observation takes practice. Seek out opportunities to observe different social or work situations, pay attention to how people interact with each other, and reflect on your observations so that you can learn from them. With time and practice, your ability to observe will become second nature—allowing you to make informed decisions that will bring success in any endeavor.

The Power of Looking Up

Years ago, I met a father whose daughter struggled with drug addiction. He tried everything to help her—he paid for rehab, he encouraged her, he took her to counseling, and he even threatened her with tough love by telling her that he would send her away.

He returned home one day to find her gone. While he was away at work, she just left. She didn't even leave a note.

The man lived in anguish for two months, barely able to walk the short distance to his office each day. Brokenhearted, he felt like he'd failed as a parent. Every day, with earphones blaring in his ears to drown out images of worst-case scenarios, he walked to and from work in a zombie-like state.

Then, just when he was about to lose all hope, his daughter came home. His heart flooded with relief. He expected to be furious but was just anxious to know what happened. *What was she doing? Where did she go?*

First, he told her, he needed to know where she'd gone. "I looked everywhere for you," he said.

She stared at him blankly. "Dad," she said slowly. "I saw you every day."

"What? What are you talking about? You've been gone for over four weeks!"

"I was sitting by the newspaper stand down the street. Dad, you walked right past me every day."

The man's eyes welled up with tears. "I didn't even see you."

He was so anxious to find his daughter that he couldn't even see her. He rushed to work each morning, lost in his despair as he contemplated what he was doing wrong as a parent and how he was failing in life. If he had looked up and paid attention, he would have found her. If he'd listened and observed, he might have noticed how sad and withdrawn he had become in his own life. Our responsibility is not to save others, but to be present so we can think clearly and explore how to take care of ourselves so that we can be available to serve others.

When the man shared his story with me, I felt a flood of relief at the happy ending. His daughter got the help she needed and was seeing progress in her life. A stranger stopped to talk to her on the street for over two hours. He shared a story about his own battle with addiction and told her funny stories about his own daughter. He asked her questions about her hopes and dreams. He wrote an address in a blank journal and told her to write how she wants this story to begin and end. She imagined herself addiction-free, playing tennis with her dad. This stranger saw something in her, stopped to connect, and encouraged her to get help.

I was really inspired by this story. But I felt a pang of sadness, too.

I couldn't help but think of what a nightmare those months must have been for the man—and his daughter. He was a leader that reached out to me for help. He felt empty. The relationship with his daughter and a handful of issues at work had consumed his thoughts for the past several years. I knew exactly what he needed. I put him on a very strict "joy diet." I told him to keep encouraging his daughter to keep reaching out to professionals for help and drive her to meetings and appointments when she asks. Then, keep looking up. Not for the purpose of saving anyone or searching for an opportunity to be useful, but for the purpose of simply enjoying life. His soul was weak, and his heart was tired. "For 30 days," I said, "ignore achievement, goals, and problem-solving. Figure out what and who you love. Find your passions. Once you are strong, your strategic brain will kick into high gear, and it will be time to make some major changes."

Observation is a skill that can be sneaky. It seems easy, but people are not paying attention to important things in a world of distractions and competing priorities. The practice of seeing the world as a massive, interconnected web demands a conscious effort. It requires us to contemplate reality. Then, by taking in everything around us without personal judgment, we suddenly see the connections all around us.

Observing is about taking little grooves and stepping back to see how they converge into one another. Like creeks that run into rivers that eventually drain into the vast expanse of the ocean, those little pathways of listening are part of something much larger. We find that big picture through observation. And through systems thinking, we make sense of it all.

Systems thinking is a discipline of observation, defined simply as a process of looking at the world as an interconnected network. In systems thinking, we often use diagrams or maps to break down the components of any given situation. And we pay particular attention to the links between these components. Those links are the path to a shared understanding of reality.

It takes a lot of practice to find them. We must be willing to peel back our defenses and take in the world with the same open-minded hunger that my dad brought to music.

As a kid, I watched how my dad's face changed when he played the drums. He played with mastery, but also watched the band members, looked at the audience, made quirky faces, sang, and even talked when all of this was going on. He was part of a web that resulted in great entertainment.

Like a show, I recognized what was happening at that meeting, when John's ideas about faculty offices were dismissed while Joseph's random interjections earned him the respect of his peers. When people used the word *productivity*, everybody's eyes lit up.

I'd seen it, and I tested it by using the word myself. Simply by using that word, I captured the attention of everybody in the room. The key to systems thinking and observation is that I tried using the word and observed the feedback loop. There was a possibility that I could have used that same strategy and failed to get the results. So, as a keen observer, I keep testing different strategies and observing the outcomes. In systems thinking, we call this a *feedback loop*.

Too busy with their own agendas, most people prefer to close themselves off and immerse themselves in the zombie world of smartphones, calendar invites, emails, and commutes.

Who, in the meeting, puts in the effort to observe the system of choices?

Be a Henry Higher-Up

Have you ever called for tech support? Maybe you needed help with some software on your phone. Perhaps you're one of the millions who call into centers located around the country and around the world designed to handle customer service. If you have, you likely met someone we'll call Marcy Smart. Marcy exists at the first level of customer engagement— she can provide basic troubleshooting, usually asking whether you've tried turning the phone off and back on. Maybe Marcy helped you. Perhaps she didn't. If she didn't, you likely talked to Innovaté.

Innovaté has knowledge that Marcy does not. She is better trained in the workings of your device, and she has a broader scope of how customer service impacts the vision and future of the company. Innovaté once sat where Marcy did, but by working to understand the levels and systems that exist within the company, she was promoted out of Marcy's position.

Innovaté is not better than Marcy. In fact, Marcy is very smart. She just hasn't observed the systems at play. Plenty of zombies unconcerned with the systems in the world remain Marcys; they never look beyond turning the device off and back on.

Organizations have hierarchies, but rather than mere levels of power, they operate more as levels of understanding and observation. Those with the broadest view of the systems that exist within the organization are Henry Higher-Ups. This level observes how a negative customer encounter impacts the vision and values of the entire company. Like

> Organizations have hierarchies, but rather than mere levels of power, they operate more as levels of understanding and observation.

Marcy, Henry once answered calls. But unlike their zombie counterparts, when he received calls, he understood that a customer was entering into a system of support. They weren't just another angry caller he had to deal with. He was dealing with something larger than himself.

Everybody sees it. Some people stick to advising customers to turn their devices on and off, never bothering to understand how everything connects. They are unable to do what needs to be done, so they continually escalate issues and ask for help. That's the very definition of someone at a low level.

All it takes to be at a high level is to see the system. The only requirement for that kind of job is to be a systems thinker. That's it. End of list.

Many people want to make an impact on the world. Working for that next promotion, they hope to improve their workplace, gain the edge, and rake in the money. They want to help people.

All those things are contingent upon our ability to connect and observe. Through systems thinking, we can position ourselves as the people who can impact the world—and that takes more than turning the device off and back on.

An Observation about the State of the Workforce

Over the next few decades, there will be three types of companies: the ones people love, the ones people hate, and the ones no one remembers. The state of the workforce is drastically changing. The conditions, skills, opportunities, and requirements are changing so fast that, at some point, not even the best brands will be able to keep up. For some companies, the future is bright, and success is inevitable. Companies have to build, hone, and create an identity and a stable culture that focuses on happiness, agility, and higher-level thinking. According to the World Economic Forum, analytical thinking and innovation, active learning strategies, and complex problem-solving are among the top skills employees will need to face future workforce challenges. The foundation of all these skills is all about making conscious connections, in particular, observing the world and understanding the interrelated parts that make up the system.

Savor the Details

Picture a staircase, ideally one you encounter often. Focus on the color and the texture of the steps; imagine walking up one stair at a time. Think about how steep the steps are and whether any of them creak or sag. As you imagine yourself climbing upward, feel your hand on the rail or wall next to you. Is the rail typically cold, or does it tend to be closer to body temperature? Is the stairwell dark or well lit? How long does it take you to reach the top?

Now ask yourself how many steps there are.

If the last question stumped you, you're not alone. John Watson had the same reaction when Sherlock Holmes posed the question to him in Arthur Conan Doyle's *A Scandal in Bohemia.* As Holmes pointed out, Watson had seen the staircase leading up to his study hundreds of times, yet he couldn't even guess how many steps there were.

The reason is simple. To borrow Holmes's words, "You see, but you do not observe."

So many of us are like Watson. As we rush through our days, taking in only the sights that seem important at the time, we miss so many of the details around us. Our life becomes a scavenger hunt of distractions, meant to be collected and dispersed as quickly and thoughtlessly as possible.

Most of us don't know how many steps we climb as we make our way through our homes or workplaces. And why should we? Most of us never need to know that information.

On the other hand, how many pieces of information do we overlook because they don't seem important at the time? How often do we wish we'd paid more attention, faced with an urgent life dilemma and no time to gather the necessary information? How many times have we looked back on a tragedy and said, "If only someone had seen the signs before it was too late?"

Too often.

And yet, eyes glazed, we continue to march through the world complaining about the same things we've always complained about. We feel powerless to slow down the constant, overwhelming flow of information. When we should stop, breathe, and observe, we dig our heels into the ground and stay put. We tell ourselves it's technology's fault, it's just the pace of life today, our jobs are too overwhelming, our kids need too much, or our community just doesn't understand us.

We tell ourselves we're helpless.

We're not.

Several ways are available to develop your powers of observation because there are so many things to observe. We'll work through each of them.

Sherlock Holmes is a genius because he mastered an amazing combination of skills, intuition, observation, and systems thinking. We all have the capacity for genius with the right combo of daily habits. Like my dad, wandering around the world with a pair of drumsticks, we just have to practice.

Holmes practiced observing constantly. Just before he questions Watson about the steps up to the study, Holmes undertakes the type of stripped-down observational analysis that is his signature. He first comments on Watson's weight gain—a simple enough observation—before casually noting that his friend must have taken a walk in the rain shortly after giving his house girl notice that she would be fired.

Perplexed, Watson asks how he knew all this.

Holmes replies, "It is simplicity itself . . . my eyes tell me that on the inside of your left shoe, just where the firelight strikes it, the leather is scored by six almost parallel cuts. Obviously, they have been caused by someone who has very carelessly scraped round the edges of the sole to remove crusted mud from it. Hence, you see, my double deduction that you had been out in vile weather, and that you had a particularly malignant boot-slitting specimen."

In other words, based on six marks on Watson's shoes, Holmes gathers that Watson's servant must have been angry when she removed the mud — and he can think of no other reason for her careless anger than having recently been fired. Most of us wouldn't have noticed the six grooves on Watson's shoes. And, in most cases, it wouldn't matter. Holmes's observations, in that case, are little more than a parlor trick.

Think for a moment of the intense connection between these two men. Intimately attuned to the tiny changes in Watson's appearance, Holmes could pick up on even more important aspects of his friend's life. Henry Higher-Up has a lot in common with Mr. Holmes.

My own Sherlock Holmes moment came on a train in Paris when I was sitting next to a woman who only spoke French. She had a baby carriage, a long baguette, a big diaper bag, and a large purse. The baby was snug and peaceful, but tears welled in the woman's eyes. I noticed and gave her a bright smile.

Suddenly, the train lurched to a stop, sending the woman's bags flying. I quickly picked them up and flashed another big smile. She then began speaking to me in French. Not understanding a word, I listened anyway, and amazingly, I felt like I got the gist of her emotions—she was fed up with something and tired of something else. As her stop approached, she wiped her tears, took a deep breath, and smiled a huge grin. She grasped my hand and said, "*Merci*, merci, merci, thank you."

To this day, I'm not sure what I did. But she got off that train looking happier. We really connected somehow. I felt alive in the world. After she left the train, I looked around and noticed people sleeping, reading, staring into the air, or scrolling their phones. I don't know if they noticed the woman and her baby. I don't know if they even noticed me. Because I've made it a habit to attune myself to others' emotional states, tapping into this woman's pain was natural. We'd never met. But I could read her as clearly as Holmes read Watson.

Imagine being so attuned to your child's life that you notice they are smiling more—or smiling less. How could you use that information to connect without judging?

"How are you?" you might ask. "Want to hang out tonight?"

If they say, with a smile, "Nope, I'm good," you might think they're in love. Maybe they've made a new close friend or are enjoying an after-school activity.

If, on the other hand, they say, "Yeah, that sounds good," then you've learned something very valuable about their need for connection, allowing you to react to what you observed without prying for details.

Recent studies have shown that feeling seen and heard are two of the greatest needs humans have. Have you ever thought about how powerful it is to take note of all the little details in a person's life? By paying attention to their body language, speech, and emotions, we can gain valuable insights into what motivates them—and use these observations to establish meaningful connections.

It may seem trivial at first, but mastering the art of noticing can open up a world of possibilities for personal growth. We can look closely at how people interact with each other and draw parallels between our own lives for lessons we can learn. A single detail about someone could be the key to unlocking your potential for success.

Think back to when we were babies—although limited in our abilities, we demanded much love and attention from those around us. What if we carried that same level of connection with us as adults? What if being attuned to others' needs wasn't seen as nosiness, but rather an alternative way to show love?

A study by the *Harvard Business Review* found that when people feel genuinely connected and cared for, they have improved performance at work and higher levels of job satisfaction.[1] Imagine what would happen if conscious connection was a movement! People feeling visible, heard, validated, and empowered—couldn't that change the world? So, let's start a movement: notice the little things about people and share your own story without judging or making assumptions. See others authentically for who they are, create meaningful conversations around that, and unlock your full potential!

The Art of Zooming Out

Have you ever engaged in people-watching? Have you silently observed people's public behaviors on your way to work, from a window at home, or while sitting in a restaurant? How some parents interact with their children, how the person at Starbucks serves you your coffee? Do you stop to notice them? As you move through your day, are you aware of the people in your surroundings as people, or do you sidestep around them like furniture?

Whatever your answer, I recommend consciously developing a people-watching habit. This kind of observation is one of the most powerful leadership and life habits we can adopt. As a note, you are not creepily staring at people, but simply looking up and putting away distractions as you take in your surroundings.

I've visited countless work environments and noticed something pervasive, particularly in the corporate workspace. While some people are present in the moment, looking around and taking in their surroundings, most people's heads are elsewhere. They're completely zoned out.

The daily habit of ignoring others isn't serving anyone well, but the challenge is especially great for those in leadership roles who are supposed to motivate others.

How do we wake up, so we can wake up other people? How do we *zoom out to see the entire picture?*

The answer is—you guessed it—observation.

Many of us *think* we're observing when we're really judging and assessing. Too often, we don't stop and reflect on the information available in our environment. We usually have all the information we need to overcome our problems. However, solutions elude us when we haven't taken the time to process that information—to understand how it links with other information.

As a leadership and development trainer, I've discussed leaders' problems and challenges in every conceivable environment. The same challenges come up repeatedly, and my responses are equally consistent.

Like John, Joseph, and Sarah's colleagues, people are always concerned about productivity and time. "I can't get anything done!" they complain. "Every time I walk into my office, the goals change, then I have to attend a dozen more meetings!"

When I talk to higher-level leaders, they word their concerns differently. "I need to get my team committed to the vision," they say. "I need to motivate them to do more with less."

I always ask a version of one question: "What are you choosing to do—or *not* do—that is impacting your ability to reach your goals?" I encourage them to quickly answer with one behavior that might be affecting their outcomes the most. Are there one or two things connected to the changes they desire?

Whether that goal is finishing their own work, motivating their team, balancing their lives, or earning that promotion, I ask the same questions: What are you choosing? What are you *not* choosing?

I ask these questions because most leaders have been observing and judging without making the connections attached to their mission or vision. With a bit of reflection, the observations they've already made will fall into place, a network of ideas mapped onto their world just beneath the surface.

They just have to tap into that reservoir of observation.

The wisdom is there. It demands effort and conscious connection.

Are You Wasting Your Mornings?

In the business world, a lot of time, money, and energy is spent on SWOT analyses, which are formal evaluations that explore a business's strengths, weaknesses, opportunities, and threats. Companies around the world use these analyses to make foundational decisions, relying on the results to determine whether to open new branches or close old ones, hire or fire workers, invest in acquisitions, or reorganize entirely.

There are fundamental limitations of applying a SWOT analysis, particularly for leaders who haven't done the work of observation. If SWOT analyses aren't conducted honestly and objectively, they're useless—simply a pseudoscientific justification for actions we'd already planned to take.

Consider a situation I encountered a few years ago. As part of a company-wide analysis, I was introduced to two middle managers. We will call them Mark and Mary. Their names were similar, but otherwise, they were incredibly different people. Mary arrived at work every day at seven o'clock, two hours early for the official workplace start time. Dressed in a conservative skirt or pants suit, she hustled into the office with her lunchbox and briefcase—color coordinated, of course—at her side. More organized than almost anyone else in the office, Mary began her day by sorting her email inbox, clearing the messages down to zero if she could, while she sipped a can of Diet Coke through a straw. While she had a quick smile when office friends approached, she tended to be quiet and kept mostly to herself.

Mark couldn't have been more different. Almost every day, he misplaced something—his car keys, coffee mug, or glasses. He was incredibly outgoing, stopping to chat with every employee along the path from the building's entrance to his desk. For 45 minutes at the beginning of every day, he wandered through the office and stopped to talk with anybody who made eye contact.

Mark didn't even have a to-do list, let alone a 36-point daily plan like Mary. And when I first glanced at his computer screen, I laughed out loud—he had 3,608 unread messages in his inbox, and the computer's desktop was so packed with documents that the icons literally overlapped.

Mary had always been described as a diligent, thoughtful worker. Accomplishing her goals with integrity, she spent a lot of time thinking about how she could make herself more attractive to senior partners, hoping for a promotion and a raise. Mark seemed to move through the office on instinct, taking things as they came.

And then came time for promotions.

File box overflowing, Mark schlepped his belongings from his middle management office to one with a gorgeous view of the Manhattan skyline.

Mary remained at her tidy, well-kept desk in the same role she'd had for years.

The decision of who to promote seemed utterly counterintuitive to many of the company's workers, Mary included. But it made perfect sense to me.

All the World's a System

Offices are systems.

Faculty meetings are systems.

Musical ensembles are systems.

Scientific experiments are systems.

Families are systems.

Neighborhoods are systems.

None of us know the details of how these systems work until we're dropped in the middle of them. Even then, they can seem confusing and inconsistent.

Like biologists with unknown specimens, we must inspect them with an open, curious spirit. That means quieting our minds, derailing the constant, inaccurate feedback loop that plays in our minds, and drowning out the music of our lives.

Consider the following thoughts:

- "Joseph just doesn't like me. That's why he always steals my attention in faculty meetings."
- "It doesn't matter how many steps are in my house. What matters is that I don't have a solid connection with my son!"
- "Of course Mark got the promotion. Everybody loves him. I'm just an unlikable person. Or it might be because he is a man."

They are self-centered feedback loops. No matter what we take in from the world around us, if we let ourselves get bogged down in our own personal biases, we'll always find ourselves stuck. We will struggle to understand what's real and what matters. Our observations are filtered through the lens of our inner chatter.

Systems have observable rules that aren't about us. When we finally internalize that reality, we free ourselves from the chains of the nightmare. Marcy Smart becomes Henry Higher-Up by understanding the rules.

It takes work. To begin, we have to make observation a habit. Then we have to shed the limitations of self-serving feedback loops, tapping into the intuition we've built as observers. Only then can we incorporate a high-level understanding of systems thinking into our own lives, allowing us to recognize and avoid negative patterns. When we finally achieve that level of observation, we can embrace the connections around us, reinforce positive action, and change our lives for the better.

So how do we begin to do that work? Systems thinking tells us that we must pay attention to three things. First, we must *observe our place in the world.* Observing the world means understanding where we fit. How do our roles as parents, leaders, and community members place us within the context of our world? Who else is in the world? How are they connected to us? Second, observing our place in the world means observing how we *impact those around us.* Have we used our place in the world to create a more caring, just society? Have we used our role as a leader to create positive change in our organization? In a sense, observing can be compared to reflection. What we say and what we do impact our family, our team, our community, and the world. Finally, we must realize *how others impact us.* Observing our impact on the world means observing the way it, and the people in it, impact *us.* Have we fully recognized how others' work makes our lives better? Do we understand the sacrifices others have made for us? Can we see the acts of selflessness that create ripple effects in our world?

Observing your world means taking it off autopilot and stopping the zombie-like trance through daily life. When we grow aware of what goes on around us, we find space for discovery—it's the difference between understanding the world as background noise and committing to intellectual and emotional engagement. As conscious observers, we incorporate ourselves into our surroundings. We become more attentive to our presence in the world. Less isolated and alone, we suddenly learn to live.

If you've ever stooped over a microscope, you understand this intuitively. You peer into the lens, furrowing your brow at those little squiggles and circles, gel-like organisms invisible to the naked eye. At first, you have no idea what you're looking at. You don't even know how to adjust the instrument to make the view clearer. Eventually, you learn.

Scientists weren't born knowing how to use a microscope, and my dad wasn't born understanding music.

If you keep looking, though, the answer will emerge. Eventually, we master the skill of observation. And then we don't even have to strain anymore. At some point, we discover that we are conscious of the connections all around us. We just know the answer.

We *feel and see* the connection.

It's All about You, and Not about You at All

Let's return to the story of Mark and Mary with one simple question. Why did Mark get the promotion?

Stop for a moment, step back, and honestly ask yourself why.

Like the grooves on Watson's shoes, the high-pitched tinkle of a Count Basie riff, or even the caller asking for help with a phone, all the clues are there. And while I've thrown in some red herrings—just to make the exercise a bit more challenging—the answer is relatively simple. Yet, when I present this scenario to clients, most are stumped.

"Maybe Mark was just friendlier," they hypothesize. "More likable."

That's undoubtedly true, but, in this case, that was not the reason for his promotion.

"He just *acted like a leader,*" others say.

Could be, but while some leaders act like Mark, others act like Mary.

"Did Mark build better relationships with the partners?" they asked, as many start to dig deep for the answer I have in mind.

As a systems thinker, I find it likely that all of these factors played a role in the promotion, yet there is one thing that might have tipped the scales.

The best observers ask good questions. They dig deeper into details that may reveal the "big idea." "What kinds of things did Mark talk about during those 45 minutes every morning while Mary was checking email?"

That's the question that unlocks the riddle—Mark spent those "wasted" 45 minutes learning more about his company. By chatting with people around the office, he learned about employee satisfaction. He listened when people complained to him, so he knew all about what wasn't working in the office. He understood his coworkers' goals and gathered their visions for the organization, their departments, and their own personal careers. And, as he did, he internalized the system at the company's foundation. The most important conversations Mark had during his mornings were with leaders that were setting the agenda for the next fiscal year. The priorities were morale, retention, and building company culture. So, we later learned that Mark decided to put 45 minutes on his calendar to build company culture. He understands leadership. He gets the system. He wasn't just chatting. He was observing and making connections. He was letting feedback loops drive his choices.

Mary did a lot of great work, but she was so caught up in her own tasks that she failed to step back and evaluate the big picture. Like Watson, she focused on what she *thought* would solve the problem—her own behaviors. She came to work early, turned in her work predictably and on time, worked through lunch, and made sure to always stay too busy to do the things she assumed were a waste of time. A highly productive worker, Mary was a valued member of the company's team. She just wasn't tuned in to the intelligence of the system.

I work with many people like Mary, high achievers who feel confident and even bullheaded about how they approach work. They seem to spin their wheels and find themselves trapped in a confusing cycle of frustration. Why? Because they're too focused on themselves. They try to force their worlds into alignment by zooming in, falsely believing that if only they can control every second of every minute of every day, they'll finally get what they want. And, they are way too confident, without sufficient observation, in their capacity to determine what matters.

Business decisions aren't based on single seconds; neither are major life choices like marriage, children, buying a home or car, moving across the country, or taking a well-deserved vacation. And social issues are certainly not solved by examining a single action. In every area of our lives, the most significant decisions are made based on observing systems *as systems*. They require us to zoom out to see how the seconds, minutes, hours, and days work together to paint a bigger, comprehensive picture of how the world works now—and how it *should* work in the future. You simply can't gather that information by sitting at your desk, going through your emails. So, Mark got the promotion and Mary was left behind.

Beyond Mark and Mary, there's a third entity in the room—the elephant. When I tell this story, people often ask whether gender bias was also at play in this promotion. It's undeniably possible. The only way to know for sure is to observe, try new behaviors to test assumptions, and uncover what's real. I've coached many women around changing their approach, getting a seat at the leadership table, then using their power and influence to impact the system of inequities.

Throughout the process, the necessity of observation never goes away. We must constantly pay attention to others' reactions to our new behaviors and approaches, consistently asking whether our actions are helping to enact change.

Our job is to identify those things that impact the system by zooming out and then zooming in on what we can control and influence. If our feedback loops uncover inequities, the system does not change. We attempt to change it by summing up a complex issue into a single statement: "This place is unfair." We must listen and observe, identifying the web of details to make micro-choices that drive macro changes.

As we've seen so far in this chapter, you can't gather that information by focusing on yourself. You are a part of a larger system. Tightening your jaw and forcing everything to fit a predetermined structure is a recipe for failure.

The world can be complicated and challenging. The path of the leader is about focusing on self-improvement, growth, and supporting others through knowing, being, and doing. Judgment is not keen observation. Your opinions may not align with reality. Do you want someone to patronize you and agree with you to avoid conflict? Or, are you interested in progress and action? When it comes to other people, we judge others, getting caught up in what they think and do wrong. When it comes to self-reflection, we either let ourselves off the hook or hold ourselves to ideals and standards that deplete our joy and energy. We find ourselves making millions of assumptions about how the world works until we are no longer observing and seeing what is real. The solution is to commit to a life of learning. If we see life as an expedition where we get to explore epic routes, we will master concrete observations, collect feedback about how things operate in the world, and find a shared truth.

> We find ourselves making millions of assumptions about how the world works until we are no longer observing and seeing what is real.

We can also accept the existence of paradoxical truths. One of which is an age-old leadership paradox that we can embrace. It is about you, but not about you at all.

Shift to Observe Your Power

Janice smiled into her computer camera, making warm eye contact even on Zoom. This wasn't the first time we'd met. We corresponded several times since she first attended a talk I was giving to a "women in leadership" group in Washington, DC. I was glad to see her, of course, but I was also curious. Every time we spoke—even through emails or texts—I saw her growth.

As she logged on that day, though, something looked different. A fire still burned behind her eyes, but it reflected something other than passion. Determination? Anger?

As soon as we'd greeted each other, she shared her screen.

"It's my letter of resignation," she said.

I was shocked! While I knew she'd struggled with some of her coworkers from time to time, I couldn't believe she could have shifted her goals so dramatically. She'd been a fierce career professional with every possibility of advancing in her firm.

"What's going on?" I asked.

She told me how my trainings had opened her eyes—how they'd changed her—and that after nearly 15 years of riding the same elevator, with mostly the same people for that entire time, she was ready to move on. Rarely had the others, all fellow employees, and all men, ever engaged with her in conversation. Not so much as the obligatory small talk, let alone any attempt at a true connection. She was done.

"It all came from living my values, Talia," she said. "It took a lot of work, but I can finally see how undervalued I am at my company. Nobody pays attention to me—I never get invited to lunch or out for drinks. People don't even acknowledge me in the elevator." She paused a moment, taking a deep breath. "I've had it. I'm going to quit and find my dream somewhere else."

Janice's decision is not for everyone. I want to make it explicitly clear that quitting your job is not part of the LOVE system (listen, observe, value, engage)—and if your resignation is fueled by discouragement, complaints, and anger, it's crucial that you keep practicing conscious connections until you're certain of your purpose. If resigning is the right choice, you'll feel pulled by your purpose—not pushed by stress. You'll be moving toward conscious connections, not running from an opportunity to practice LOVE.

For Janice, a long, intentional journey through the LOVE cycle helped her listen to herself, and she grew a lot personally. By listening to herself, she'd determined her true goals and how to reach them. She connected with her inner voices until they became a chorus pushing her forward. Then she focused on her observation skills. We often spoke of how she looked for the systems that bind us together. She marveled at how her work life, nature, and even her private life all came together to form her world. I especially liked it when she told me about how she spends an hour every day on the balcony overlooking the street and just listens to the city around her. She truly made her way along the journey toward LOVE.

Still, she never spoke about her job in a way that led me to believe that she was on the brink of quitting.

Looking her in the eyes, I wondered about her life, so I gently inquired, "When you were speaking, I was just wondering about your childhood and some commonalities of being overlooked in the past. When things like being ignored happens, does it remind you of anything?"

"Well, maybe," she said tentatively. I didn't give her the reaction she expected from the resignation letter, and now she seemed on shakier ground. "I am a middle child with lots of siblings, so I have always kind of been ignored, I guess . . . My childhood was pretty tough. I had to deal with a lot of drama."

"I see," I said, smiling reassuringly. "What if I gave you a quick shift?" I sensed her hesitance, so I continued, "To make sure there isn't another way of looking at the issue. Just a quick value realignment."

She shrugged. "Who could say no to that, I guess! Go for it."

"Remind me of your values, Janice," I said.

The questioning look on her face told me she was curious. "You mean like loyalty, teamwork, and creativity?"

"That's perfect. Got it," I said as if I just cracked a code.

Since we weren't on stage, we faced each other on the camera, but I still stepped into her life—I do this relatively frequently for clients. Since I suspected—and Janice confirmed—that some childhood insecurities were coming into play, I started there. As I opened my shift, I said, *Wow, I'm a professional now. I am worthy and have a lot of value to add.*

Janice was beaming, and I continued.

"Teamwork is important to me, but the reason why it's important is not because of what the team does for me, but how excited I get about what I can

do for the team. I love being creative. I like people to notice my creativity. I really enjoy being able to show my talents and be acknowledged for them. When I was young, I had to work hard to be acknowledged and seen. Yet, I have always known that I have what it takes to add value. I am excited about finding creative ways to give myself the kind of validation that I need.

"I'm a team player. I am awesome. I am creative. And just like that, I can create things that add value to a team. I can create a way to meet my need to feel heard and seen. I do not need to depend on others to give it to me." I paused a moment and smiled. *"Maybe I've been looking for love in all the wrong places."*

At that, Janice erupted into laughter. It was good to see her break into her usual self again. There was more to shift, though, so I continued. *"Maybe my purpose is not to be seen or heard by this group of people. My purpose is to see and to hear, and to show them what it looks like to acknowledge and honor people."*

I saw the spark return. This time I knew what it was. It was pure power, relief, and determination. Firmly, with an assuredness that hadn't been there moments ago, she simply responded, "Oh, Talia." She sighed, a smile turning up the corner of her mouth. "Yes, you're right."

We chatted a bit more, then ended the call.

Just a few months later, I saw her again. I was eager to hear more about her job. I didn't have to wait long. As soon as the Zoom room opened, I saw that she was holding a printed piece of paper. "It's the letter of resignation I showed you last time," she said. "I printed it."

I was curious to hear about how the shift might have changed her perspective. I felt certain that the shift was just what she needed to align with a value-based choice. If she'd printed the letter, she must have decided to go through with the resignation.

I raised my eyebrows. "I see you are still ready to—"

Before I could finish, she ripped the paper in half.

She decided to double down on her journey toward LOVE—to make sure she was living her values—and to use them to guide how she listened, observed, and engaged. When she began to express her values, she found herself connecting with her coworkers in ways that she had never thought possible. As she listened to herself, she started to shift her identity. She began to align her thoughts with her values. She practiced gently guiding herself— not out of fear or sadness or disappointment but out of a sincere desire to connect, to give, and spread value. And as she supported those around her, everyone succeeded.

Her company noticed as well.

She began reflecting on the journey. "For so long, I thought it was this organization that was the problem." I knew where she was going. "Then I came to my first class and learned what it meant to be a mission-driven professional."

"Don't you feel empowered and in control?" I asked.

"Yes, exactly!" she gushed, coming alive with the idea. "I wanted to be listened *to*. But I realized that I wasn't listening to *others*. And I learned so much about people and the business when I finally started paying attention to the right things."

"So, how did that go?" I asked. "What did you learn?"

"I learned that I'd closed off the very connections I wanted to foster," she replied. "I listened only to protect myself, never listening to give back. So here's what I did. Each morning before walking out of my house, I would tell myself, *Today, I'm going to let go of my need to be seen. I will be the spearhead of creating a culture—I will show others how to live with LOVE. I'm going to celebrate my team members. I'm going to fill people with such good feelings and thoughts that they're not going to know what hit them. And at the end of the day, I'm going to walk out of my office with my head held high."*

"Because you don't need that validation anymore, right?" I asked.

"Right! It's almost a little cynical, but I thought to myself, I don't need them to lift me up. I'm good."

She went on to tell me all about her growing relationships at work. She was closer with her own team than ever before. She began developing relationships with the leaders of other divisions within her firm. It was those connections—and the benefits that resulted—that had caught the attention of the CEO. Less than a year later, we met again.

"I want to share my screen again, Talia."

I raised my eyebrows, and she laughed.

When the document popped up, it was a letterhead template. And at the top, it read "Janice Brown, Senior Vice President of Marketing." Another huge promotion. Another case for LOVE.

Can you relate to Janice? It can be frustrating to feel like your hard work and dedication are still not getting you the results that you want.

Janice is a businesswoman working in an intense, fast-paced environment. Despite her skills and expertise, she felt ignored and diminished by her leadership team and colleagues. Rather than blame others or give up, Janice decided to make a change, starting with herself.

She began to focus on self-reflection and recognized when she was seeking validation from unreliable sources. She then shifted this energy toward positive affirmations about herself and how she could uplift and encourage herself to serve and lead.

Janice's determination paid off—as soon as she changed her attitude toward people around her and started actively engaging in meaningful conversations with empathy, she noticed a shift in how she perceived others. Soon enough, she received the recognition that she had been striving for!

The takeaway here is simple: connection through service-oriented attitudes and self-love can go a long way when it comes to achieving success through conscious connections. Every connection becomes an opportunity for expansion.

Observe to Expand

Every connection becomes an opportunity for expansion.

Bev Harding has taught tenth-grade English at a small school in northwestern Pennsylvania since the late '90s. Known for her impressive collection of brightly colored scarves and her penchant for quoting Shakespeare, she might seem more at home in an art or theater classroom, but she loves English. As a child, she often felt isolated and alone. Books were her escape.

Most days after school, she'd walk toward her house, a little bungalow in the middle of a quiet, tree-lined block. Instead of turning right toward her front door, she'd hang a left toward the library. Those shelves of old, well-loved books might as well have been her home back then.

She chose a career in education because she wanted to give kids the gift of reading. After years in the classroom, a lot of people have watched her read from her beloved *Romeo and Juliet*. Until recently, she'd never seen *herself* read those beloved passages.

For years, every time a new teacher approached the principal or teaching coach for advice on how to captivate students, they were sent to Bev. During observations, the fledgling teachers sat in the back of the classroom and observed not only what Bev said, but also how she arranged her classroom, how she grouped her students, how she structured the lesson, and what techniques she used to keep order. Teaching is much more than just presenting the material. Bev knew that intuitively for years. And then she had the opportunity to observe herself.

In 2013, her district piloted the Best Foot Forward Project, a Harvard-designed intervention designed to "de-privatize" instruction. The program replaced teacher evaluations—traditionally in-person, drop-in observations by school administrators—with teacher-created videos. Teachers who participated in the study recorded as many instructional periods as they wanted, then chose which ones to share with the administration. The idea was to de-privatize teaching, allowing other teachers to see what went on in the most successful classrooms.

As it turned out, these videos had another, even more beneficial, purpose. They allowed the teachers to watch *themselves* teach. Because the video captured the whole classroom, it allowed them to see things they missed while they were focusing on instruction—the student who passed a note when Bev turned to write something on the board, the student distracted by something outside the classroom window, and even the student who laughed, genuinely, at one of Bev's jokes. She'd missed all these things in the moment.

There was one thing that truly captivated Bev as she watched the video of her classroom. At the far corner of the classroom, a student bundled in a red hoodie stared unflinchingly at a poster Bev had hung on the wall years earlier. "Your attitude determines your direction," it read in big, bright, blocky letters. The poster was positioned just below the air conditioning vent. With each new puff of air, the poster flapped, threatening to pull itself off the wall. And that student in the red hoodie seemed content to watch the poster, missing out on class materials.

Bev had been teaching in that classroom for years—and that poster hung there for nearly as long. Over time, it separated itself from the wall. And she'd become immune to its dangling corner. A little pellet of sticky tac was all it took to remedy the distraction, an absurdly simple fix for a problem she hadn't even noticed. Her years in the classroom had made her a better teacher. They'd also prevented her from seeing some of the nuances of her classroom environment. While teaching, she realized that she was so engrossed in the subject matter that she failed to fully engage with her students.

Bev's experience may seem like a trivial example in a book about changing the world, but that's the thing about this major undertaking. It happens through small changes.

When Bev watched that video, she saw something she'd never noticed. The other teachers saw it too. So did the administrators and the Best Foot Forward researchers. In a way, it was the same thing my dad discovered all those years earlier. It is also like what led Arthur Conan Doyle to invent Sherlock Holmes and continues to help the Henry Higher-Ups of the world advance. What Bev saw when she watched that video far exceeded the details—a passed note, a giggle, and a flapping poster. She saw a system.

The students in the classroom were only students when they entered that classroom—before that, they'd been friends, secret crushes, troublemakers, worried daughters, and part-time fast-food workers. And the classroom wouldn't have been called a classroom if it weren't in the middle of a school and filled with desks. There is a distinction between talking and teaching. If you research "best definition of teaching," you will find the words *engage, enable,* and *process.* Bev talked about Shakespeare all the time, but after observing, she deepened her understanding of what it means to teach.

Everyone and everything in that classroom was connected, and when even one tiny detail went wrong—a bright blue poster with a forgotten motivational quote sloppily hanging—things didn't quite click.

Bev was an excellent teacher, but there was room for improvement. And while that improvement seemed totally separate from her teaching methods, it wasn't insignificant—not for that student in the red hoodie.

What if we were all part of the Best Foot Forward Project? What if, like Bev, we all had the opportunity to observe ourselves within our environments? Picture the world if we all had to reflect in such a direct and dramatic way as watching ourselves on camera lead others. I can think of no surer way to rid the world of zombies. If we were forced to see the results of our actions—or, better yet, our inaction—would we ever go on autopilot again?

Observation is transformative. It is the essence of being present in the world and shines a light on the role we play in it. All training in systems thinking, feedback loops, and observations will give you a view of how a ripple of impact transforms the world. That is how we build teams and communities. We observe each other and make tiny changes that result in big collective results.

> Systems thinking is how LOVE saves the world, and it all begins with you, observing the feedback loops of four powerful habits. Every connection is an opportunity for expanding your view of the world and elevating your purpose.

Pull Back the Curtain

Observation is a critical component of success in any worthy endeavor. Active observation skills are essential for effective leadership in any role. Whether in corporate, nonprofit, government, or small business contexts, at work or at home, observation is a useful tool for clear communication and direct action.

Passive participation in our experiences limits our understanding of how our choices impact our emotions and decisions. We often react to the behavior of others without considering why or the strategy behind what evokes our responses. Fortunes are spent by advertisers to capture our attention and manipulate our emotions. They hire skilled and active observers to analyze their strategies. For example, I once saw a commercial in which a celebrity took a big bite out of a bar of soap. I was intrigued to know what it was advertising and watched the commercial until the end. It turned out to be for a food delivery service. As an active observer, I was more fascinated by the strategy to engage viewers and hold their attention than the lure of a food delivery app. Passive participants, on the other hand, watch the commercial until the end, download the app, get distracted by other things, and then wonder why they're so unfocused.

Active observers are aware of how their environment, relationships, and communication choices impact their decisions and emotions. They intentionally choose how to act, relate, and engage. To be effective leaders, we must shift from passive participation to active observation.

Sitting in the audience engrossed in a motivational speaker's message, you can't help but be inspired—the speaker has chosen the best stories, perfected the most passionate delivery, and made dozens of other choices to engage their audience. And yet, when you hear a good speaker, those choices—the little pauses or gestures—are the furthest thing from your mind. Instead you think about, and even feel, the message. This is fine, of course; we want to experience the impact of deliberate and conscious choices. However, when it comes time to improve our skills, we want to actively observe choices so we can be inspired to use them. We want to create our own toolbox of inspiring and energizing choices.

Observation is not about forcing our environment to fit into our preconceived vision of the world—it's not a process that flows from us outward to others. Instead, when we observe, we invite an opportunity to improve everything about who we are and explore a limitless pool of possibilities.

My father learned to make sense of music and identified the parts of the system that resulted in great entertainment. The energy was infectious, and audiences loved and enjoyed the results. I made the connection between my father's approach to music and the study of systems. Then I explored ways I could use this approach in school, work, parenting, and relationships. I, then, share these connections with you.

Sherlock Holmes's observational talent was so fascinating that it made the story a legend. It unearths our deep internal desire to notice things—to demonstrate extreme intelligence. And, although being hyper-observant may come easier to some than others, we can all get significantly better at seeing our surroundings from multiple angles and perspectives, leading us to new conclusions.

I often suggest a quick trick to get Holmes-level observation talent: Ask the right questions:

- What do I see?

- What don't I see?

- How are the things I see related to a result?

- How is the thing I'm observing a part of something bigger?

- Can I see this situation, problem, or visual from multiple experiences or perspectives?

At first, it might feel awkward to run through a list of questions all the time. However, as we continue to practice this approach, our observation skills naturally sharpen. Soon we put the pieces together effortlessly and begin to see opportunities and possibilities. It will feel like magic.

Sherlock Holmes's observational powers sometimes seemed like a magic trick. He observed other people's appearances and behaviors. He used his observations to communicate care and interest to Watson. He shared what he saw to build one of the strongest friendships in literature. And this is the most crucial aspect of observation: it connects us with others.

Mark made connections based on the things he learned about his coworkers. As he made his morning rounds, he saw common themes among people, shoring up the foundation of the company's systems and culture. Bev observed herself carefully. She was committed to adjusting her approach so that her students could focus on connecting and learning.

Become a *story collector* and a *connections chef* to curate precious world-changing ideas and life-changing relationships. You could change the world.

Just imagine the ideas that would flow and the problems you could solve if you developed the habit of looking for meaning and connections by inviting others to share how they approach challenges and see the world. Become a *story collector* and a *connections chef* to curate precious world-changing ideas and life-changing relationships. You could change the world.

When we observe, we commit to becoming conscious of our environment. Of the grass we walk on as we cut through the park to get to work. Of the sun's warmth as we grab our shades to block the light. Of the children playing across the street, the woman talking on her phone in the stairwell, the barista who makes our morning coffee, and the custodian who empties our office trashcan.

Observation is about all those things—and it's about developing a conscious understanding of how those things connect. Our body is a part of something much greater than ourselves. We are a single building block in the entire natural world, and observation can strengthen our bonds with one another. All we have to do is use our observations strategically to practice LOVE as we move through the world together.

The nightmare can only prevail if we can't see. Blocking our vision, it prevents us from seeing how others around us could advance our vision of the dream. The nightmare hides those who are already listening and learning; it makes true observation seem impossible. Remember, though, that there are others out there, people attuned to the world's suffering—people who see a larger purpose for observation that goes well beyond judgment, evaluation, and complaint. For them, observation is about stepping up and taking meaningful action.

The LOVE system can help you see the world through a master's eyes. Pull back the curtains and go behind the scenes of your life, work, and society.

Commit to consciously joining the world and you'll receive that energy back tenfold—you'll suddenly find the clarity to know who you are and what you value, and you'll discover the joy of connecting with the world around you.

This one habit, practiced consistently over the next year, will yield you the benefits of leadership mastery that would take 10,000 hours to build. According to research referenced in *Outliers* by Malcolm Gladwell, it takes 10,000 hours of intense practice and study to truly master a skill. Digging deeper into this research, a great teacher is a part of the mastery system. The LOVE system can help you see the world through a master's eyes. Pull back the curtains and go behind the scenes of your life, work, and society. You have been in the audience watching the show. It is time to become a student of life who sees the work, the time, the struggle, and the joy of the process. You, then, will understand the parts of the system that make a masterpiece production. What is a masterpiece? It is observing and understanding the pieces of something that you and others deem worthy and outstanding. It is mastering the art of observing the pieces that make up our experiences together. As we evolve from mere observation to recognizing our values, we use what we observe to create and facilitate the alignment of those values with more ambitious goals. Our values then prioritize our actions based on the information that both we hear and see.

TAKEAWAYS

In this chapter, we've learned about the significance of active observation and how we can wake up and be alive in our world. Observation is a powerful tool for anyone interested in becoming an effective leader, making conscious connections, and expanding their worldview. Active observation helps us to wake up and be more mindful of the environment around us and its potential.

Observation sharpens systems thinking.
Observation supports confident decision-making.

Below are key ideas to take with you:

- **Improve relationships.** Give your friends and family, or co-workers and team members your full, undivided focus. Simply by taking the time to notice feelings, body language, and verbal clues, we can adjust our approach to have more effective interactions.

- **Zoom out.** To be an active participant in our world, we must be able to zoom out to see the big picture. We must be willing to crawl out of our own minds and take in what's happening around us. Instead of merely seeing the world, we should make connections and observe it.

- **Make observation a habit.** Take in the world around you. As you make your morning commute or hop on a virtual meeting, note how many people are around. Is it different on certain days? What are they doing? How are they behaving? People-watching is a great tool for practicing observation in our daily lives.

- **Integrate systems thinking.** To be a keen observer is to be a systems thinker and a strategist. We must realize that the world and everyone in it is interconnected. Every group within the world is a system. An office, a classroom, a team, a household—all of these are systems. Each person within a system impacts every other person and the system as a whole. To be able to make informed decisions in the future, you must learn how to observe the systems that you're part of and understand the big picture. With this information, you can make decisions that are aligned with company objectives and have a better understanding of how your contributions affect the larger system.

- **Ask the right questions to sharpen your observation skills.**

  - What do I see?

  - What don't I see?

  - How are the things I see related to a result?

  - How is the thing I'm observing a part of something bigger?

  - Can I see this situation, problem, or visual from multiple experiences or perspectives?

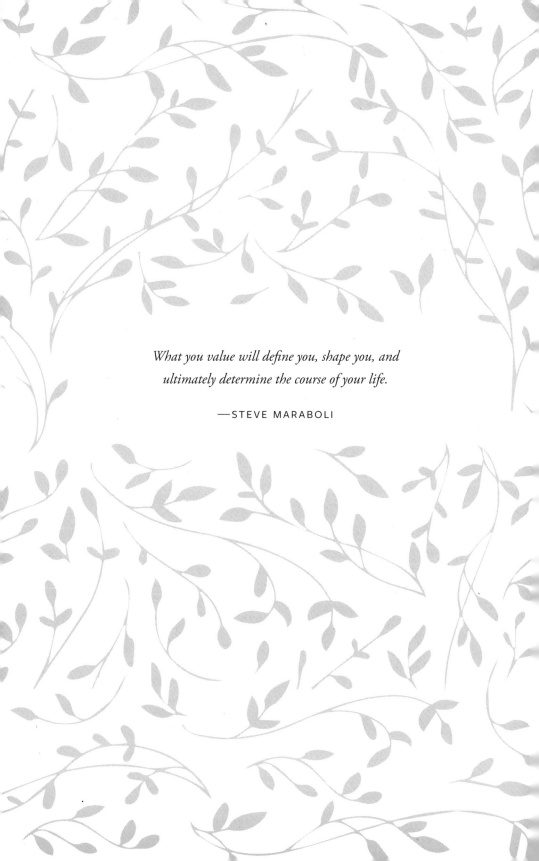

What you value will define you, shape you, and
ultimately determine the course of your life.

—STEVE MARABOLI

CHAPTER FOUR

VALUE

___

Weighing Your Options

I felt like a gnat circling his face.

"Grab me some coffee and meet me in my office," the overconfident CEO said to me, waving his hand as though he were shooing me away like an annoying insect. Without a second thought, he turned on his heel and retreated into his office.

I just stood there, stunned. As I turned to go—I wasn't sure where—I noticed my hands shaking. A hot rage boiled in my gut, and with nowhere to escape, it threatened to boil over.

I'd arrived promptly at this CEO's office to sign a big contract for my firm, ready to make an impact and prepared to add to a long list of recent wins. This big contract signing was days after completing a prestigious fellowship at Harvard and feeling on top of the world. It also meant job security for one of my employees—a mom of four boys, working from home, anxiously awaiting a report of the next tasks after securing this deal. As the CEO of my company, my job is to bring home the Tofurky. Now, on the first day of our meeting, this man—my peer and fellow CEO—quite literally waved me away. He'd dismissed me as though my only value was to bring him his coffee.

In that moment, I wondered whether Oprah had led me astray. And I don't mean her television show or magazine. I mean Oprah herself.

A few months earlier, I'd met her at the W. E. B. Du Bois Medal Ceremony. Oprah was there accepting Harvard's highest honor in the field of African American studies on behalf of the late Maya Angelou. W. E. B. Du Bois was an American sociologist, historian, and civil rights leader known for his contributions to the fight for racial justice. His leadership skills were crucial in establishing the National Association for the Advancement of Colored People (NAACP) and advocating for equal rights for African Americans in the early 20th century. Du Bois's leadership ultimately impacted society by challenging dominant narratives and promoting civil rights for marginalized communities. At this event, I'd nearly bumped into Shonda Rhimes as I made my way to my seat. Just a few tables away, Harry Belafonte was chatting with Henry Louis "Skip" Gates Jr., and I'd heard that Steve McQueen was floating around somewhere too. It was beyond a dream.

The room buzzed with energy, a steady hum of conversation echoing in Harvard's art museum. Occasionally, someone laughed a bit too loudly, increasing the air of excitement. The venue was quite grand, its antique wood benches offset by the antique woodwork surrounding the room. Above our heads, a giant crystal chandelier sparkled down on the elaborate Grecian sculptures that flanked the stage. And Oprah humbly floated around the private cocktail party.

I pinched myself. I didn't wake up.

As I approached her, she smiled big as she adjusted her large black frame glasses and greeted me with warmth and ease.

"Talia Fox," I introduced myself.

"Oprah Winfrey," she returned.

With that, we launched into a conversation so easily that I almost forgot I was speaking with the most famous media mogul in history.

I couldn't remember a time when I didn't know Oprah's name. As a young child, I remember my grandmother tuning in to her daytime talk show. My grandmother would bustle around the house while this powerful woman invited audiences around the world to tap into their courage and spirituality. Oprah had been an early adopter of the self-help movement that swept the country in the 1990s, tirelessly working to improve herself and calling all of us to do the same. In 2003, she became the world's first Black woman billionaire, an icon of culture and industry known for uplifting others with her words.

This is the woman I owe for knowing the *exact* time my son was born. In 2000, my first son was born just as her show was coming on. Oprah came on at four o'clock eastern, and yes, of course, she was on while I was in labor.

Now, at this event, she was right in front of me and I could ask her anything I wanted.

Realizing this was a once-in-a-lifetime moment, I seized my opportunity. It was 2014, and I was staring down two equally alluring career possibilities: I could accept a prestigious position at Harvard, or I could continue to invest in KUSI Global, building on the company's recent burst of success. I was torn, and I wondered what Oprah would do in my situation. So, I asked her.

This wasn't the first time I asked this question of an incredibly powerful person. For the past 10 years, I'd asked a variation of the question to many people, several other billionaires included.

"If you had my cards, what would you do?" I asked.

The results aren't just helpful to me—they reveal a lot about the other person, too. As someone who loves to know what makes other people tick, I love to watch how the question exposes their values. When you ask someone to prioritize things in *others'* lives, the normal things that hold people back—insecurity, fear, urgency, and the endless what-ifs—melt away. Suddenly, the choice becomes clearer. So I'd asked this question a lot. And, that day, I asked Oprah.

"Well, you already know what I did," she said, gaze steady and confident. "I bet on myself."

I knew she was right. And just as Oprah had urged me to do, I turned down the job in exchange for a dream.

Now, I had allowed the grab-me-some-coffee-and-meet-me-in-my-office CEO to reduce me to the size of a snail. Shame and anger burned my cheeks as my mind scrolled through the possibilities.

Should I spit in his coffee?

Should I just leave?

Should I put my middle finger up and yell, "I'm not getting you coffee! Who the hell do you think you are?! Do you know who *I* am?!"

Then I heard my grandmother's voice.

"Hold your head up high," she always said. "You are not better than anyone, but remember that no one is better than you. Don't take shit from anybody!"

My grandmother, who was the Black model on billboards across New York City. My grandmother, who was on the cover of *Jet* magazine. My grandmother, who had to fight and claw for every ounce of respect awarded to her would not want me to get that coffee.

So I weighed my options.

Align Your Actions with Your Values

There's a reason I'd asked for Oprah's advice—it's the same reason I ask all highly successful people what they would do if they were in my position. When you ask someone to make a choice, you see their values in action. Simply asking someone about their values results in all kinds of vague platitudes. People will say all kinds of things when trying to come up with the most socially acceptable response to a direct question about values. They value love. They value family. They value hard work, freedom, courage, integrity, or candor.

Most of the time, those answers aren't lies. Still, the answers will never reveal as much about a person's values as their choices. Our values aren't about what we say. They're not even about what we think or believe. Our values lie in what we *do*.

When the CEO waved his hand at me and told me to bring him coffee, I learned a lot about him. I learned a lot about myself, too.

In that moment, I thought of all the people I planned to hire as part of the contract. I remembered everyone on my team, the potential people who would come together to do meaningful work. With a pang of pride that cut through the annoyance, I recalled the mission of this man's organization. I felt so connected to what his company did.

Dropped into that situation, a hundred different people might have made a hundred different choices. Spitting in his coffee or quitting on the spot were both perfectly reasonable responses. For me, at that moment, the best choice was to put my ego aside, to take that offense, and to get him the coffee. That was the choice that best aligned with my values.

I gave him the coffee without an ounce of attitude, and we signed the contract. Then, I looked him straight in the eye and said, "I'm really looking forward to serving you well." When he smiled and started to reply, I pushed forward. "But to do that," I continued, "we need to talk about how we'll work together in a way that's mutually respectful and supports our goals."

I suggested meeting for coffee in a neutral place a few weeks later—I knew I would be more relaxed by then, the minor confrontation water under the bridge. When we met for coffee, I told him about my life, my business, and my journey. I explained the high I felt after a series of unforgettable experiences during my Harvard fellowship. As a Black woman, I'd always been taught to be humble but strong. I told him about my grandmother's words and why respect is such an important value. Looking him straight in the eye, I told him how I felt when he asked me to get his coffee.

He was, of course, very apologetic. And for the remainder of the contract—which lasted over five years—he acknowledged my work and complimented me often. I never dealt with one iota of an issue around respect with him moving forward. Perhaps even more striking, I saw him change his behavior toward other people. That kind of shift doesn't happen from shame or scolding—it can only come from a deep, internal compass, a core belief system that drives how we see the world. By finding that compass in ourselves, we can become who we want to be.

The world is a place of values, both intended and actualized.

> When just one of us chooses to look into ourselves and align our behaviors with our core beliefs—our actions with our proclaimed values—the world shifts. That kind of alignment wakes the zombies. It ejects the autopilots. It shoves us out into the beautiful, messy world and all its sparkling possibilities.

Connecting with the CEO through LOVE (listen, observe, value, engage) did that for me. And then, through clear, direct communication, I passed that alignment on to him. What if there was a mass movement to get clear on our shared values? How would your life change if you woke up each morning with this thought:

> *I know what matters most. What is good for me and good for others is the same. My values guide my choices. My choices are telling me if I am aligned with my values. Consistent alignment is my power to make dreams come true.* How might everything change? What would you say no or yes to?

When Values Collide

When you picture a US Marine, you picture someone like Jim. He sports a neatly trimmed beard speckled with flecks of white and a bulky tactical watch. Shoulders back, spine straight as a rail, he commands every room. When you meet him, the first thing you notice is his demeanor. His face is as steady as if carved in stone, stoic and strong. And yet, his expression always seems relaxed—almost soft. He observes everything around him, but that habit is so engrained it seems effortless.

Back in the early '90s, Jim served multiple tours in Desert Storm. The Marines generously rewarded his excellence in leadership and bravery, increasing his rank and positioning him as a trainer. In the context of his childhood—and his experiences of poverty, alcoholism, and domestic violence—his achievements are remarkable.

When I met Jim, he sat in the front row of a corporate leadership training I was leading for a mix of military and civilian personnel. The program was a three-day course designed to increase communication effectiveness in briefings and presentations, and Jim participated with the enthusiasm of a seasoned public speaker.

At the end of the last day of the training, I opened the floor for feedback and questions.

"Ma'am," he said, always respectful. "I'd like to offer a word of advice for future classes, if I may."

I nodded and shrugged, unsure of where his comment might go.

"As someone who gives a lot of presentations," he started, his voice oozing pride, "I encourage you to lock the door before class starts." His eyebrows raised just slightly, and a sly grin curled the corner of his mouth. "My people know," he continued, "if you're not there on time, you're not there. I'm lockin' ya out."

I leaned in, curious to know more about his thought process. "Interesting, Jim," I said. "Would you mind sharing your core values?"

"Service, integrity, and loyalty, ma'am."

It was refreshing to hear someone's values roll so easily off the tip of their tongue, so I pushed him a little more. "How does your 'locked door policy' support your values?" I asked, quickly adding, "Or, if it doesn't, what purpose does locking people out of a learning and development class serve for you and the people you typically present to?"

Around the room, other personnel cocked their heads, searching for their answer to my question. Jim thought hard for a moment, too—I could almost see the wheels spinning behind his eyes. I'd rarely seen anyone so ready to share their core beliefs. As a man who never did anything halfway, he seemed dedicated to acting on those values. And yet I suspected the team members who'd been locked out of his presentations would be surprised to hear service and loyalty at the top of his list. He was more than clear about his values. And, based on his comment, he seemed to have given a lot of thought to his actions, too.

Jim responded hesitantly, "It keeps people in line and ensures that we run a tight ship."

Careful not to be sarcastic, I replied with a direct question. "Is running a tight ship the goal of this experience?"

Professionals consistently choose to align with values where amateurs often make choices based on the emotions of the day.

Jim blinked, and I thought I saw discovery flash across his face.

The irony of my exchange with Jim is that, while I would never adopt his "closed-door policy," my classes have an unusually low rate of late arrivals. This is not an accident. I typically start my classes with my own skit that reflects two types of people, amateurs and professionals. Professionals consistently choose to align with values where amateurs often make choices based on the emotions of the day. I can't be certain of the reason, but I suspect it has to do with my approach. I set the stage to help people see how their daily choices are opportunities to honor their values. Showing up on time, unless there is a good reason not to, is an act of integrity. This equally applies to high-value meetings or an ice-cream day with the kids.

My strategy is to be engaging, to be kind, and to challenge people to think about how they want to show up. Yet they have the power to choose. Learning can only happen if the students are in the room. And since my purpose is to help students learn, shutting them out would defeat the purpose.

I choose how to run ships based on both core values and the purpose of the experience. Values should drive more conscious and deliberate choices. I suspect Jim and so many others make decisions based on habitual behaviors or personality quirks, even if the choices do not always support the goals. These habits distract us from the heart of the matter. Living life according to our purpose and values is the goal. Yet we may have to reflect on the "real" goals so we can lean on our values to achieve them.

We often make decisions based on preferences or habits when we *really* want to make value-driven decisions.

So why is it so common for our values to be misaligned with our choices? It's simple. We often make decisions based on preferences or habits when we *really* want to make value-driven decisions. If we want to make a conscious connection between our values and our daily choices, we have to practice Daily Habit Alignment (DHA). A habit is a choice we consistently make. Our values are not what we say, but what we choose.

What we choose determines who we are. We are powerful influencers with a LOVE system that will turn us into global visionaries.

Cultural Competence: A Skill and a Core Value

Cable news outlets—a primary hub of zombieland—talk constantly about values: traditional values, religious values, political values, family values, personal values.

Values aren't about what we think, feel, and believe inside. They're about how we interact with the world. Even if we clearly and effectively articulate our values, they're meaningless unless we share them with others and back those words up with life-changing actions. After all, what's the point of family values if we can't find time to connect and be present? If we aren't inviting others to participate in our lives, are we *really* valuing community? I am convinced that a large portion of the population would name respect as a core value but find themselves being disrespectful anytime someone disagrees with them. In other words, values are meaningless if we only act on them when the rest of the world is behaving according to our preferences.

Wrap your values around your life like a warm blanket. Feel secure and confident about your choices.

Values should provide a road map for our behaviors. They can help us make better choices when things are challenging. Values are the secret to a bouncy life. You will bounce back from setbacks, heal faster, forgive quickly, and have less regret. Wrap your values around your life like a warm blanket. Feel secure and confident about your choices.

The CEO who asked me to get him coffee talked on big stages about respecting and uplifting women, and he likely valued providing good services and profitability. When we talked over coffee, he had to face the conflict between his actions and core values. I do not know what drove him to ask me to get him coffee that day. Was he just having a bad day or was he stuck in a zombie moment? Maybe he completely overlooked the nuance of my background and identity that day, neglecting to consider how the request would make me feel. Or was it something else? Despite his intentions, he missed the relationship between values and actions. The intention-behavior gap isn't just about overcoming personal issues or addictions. It impacts how we interact in a world rich with different cultures, values, and preferences, and quickly becomes a widespread issue of global cultural competence.

The previous chapters have explored emotional intelligence and systems thinking as the skills that support listening and observation— the bedrocks of conscious connections. Making more deliberate choices based on core values is crucial to supporting a more inclusive society. Cultural competence is the skill that helps us translate intentions to meaningful connections.

Cultural competence refers to the ability to adapt our behaviors to reflect the intention of honoring and respecting cultural differences. This involves addressing the intention-behavior gap, where our actions might not align with our respectful intentions. On the other hand, cultural intelligence is the practice of actively listening and observing to enhance our understanding and savvy about different cultures, enabling us to adapt effectively to diverse environments. In essence, cultural intelligence expands our knowledge of how others operate in the world. While cultural competence centers on our commitment to connect consciously and respectfully with others, cultural intelligence equips us with the insights needed to make those connections more effectively.

"Culture" in this context refers to the collective habits, behaviors, beliefs, values, and traditions of a specific racial, ethnic, religious, or social group. "Competence" means having the necessary skills to navigate the complexity of our interactions with others. Most people "intend" to understand others. But, there is a gap between those intentions and behaviors.

Cultural competence and cultural intelligence are vital for social interactions, workplace environments, and education. These skills are considered essential in international diplomacy, where countries deal with different cultures and need to understand how to best work with these cultures. In a case study by the *Harvard Business Review*, it was shown that cultural competence helped a company enter a foreign market with success.[1] This was achieved by understanding how the target market was different and making changes to the company's product to cater to the cultural context. And these skills are essential for all people living in a global world—that's you!

Developing cultural competence and cultural intelligence can lead to so many benefits, such as increased productivity, better employee engagement, and a more cohesive work environment. It comes down to recognizing and adapting to cultural differences. Culturally competent people bring active empathy to their interactions with others; they consider situations from others' perspectives. When we do not understand differences, we make choices that can hurt, offend, ignore, or dismiss others. Cultural intelligence requires you to be more conscious about your observations and choices. Your goal is to learn about others. Cultural competence is your willingness to adapt your behavior to demonstrate that knowledge. So, here is why cultural competence is the keystone habit for the V in our LOVE system.

- You value respect (value).
- You know, based on cultural knowledge, that a word, topic, or choice is disrespectful to a person or culture (observe).
- You avoid that word, topic, or choice to align with your value of respect.
- You learn more about the person or culture (listen).
- You become more conscious and connected to the person and culture (engage).
- You feel smart, competent, and happy.
- Your life is more interesting and joyful.
- You get involved in a cause or movement that changes lives.
- You become a world changer.

Can it be that simple? Maybe.

An Unexpected Dinner

Layla, a first-generation American from a Pakistani background, invited her new colleague, Alice, to dinner at her home. Alice, unfamiliar with Pakistani customs, took some time before the dinner to research a bit about Pakistani etiquette and culture. She learned that it's common to bring a small gift when invited to someone's house, and also about the typical way of greeting.

When Alice arrived at Layla's home, she presented a box of assorted sweets and greeted Layla's parents with "*As-salamu alaykum*," a traditional Islamic greeting meaning "peace be upon you." Layla's parents smiled, pleasantly surprised, and responded with "*Wa alaykum as-salam*," meaning "and upon you be peace."

During dinner, Alice tried to use her right hand for eating, as she had learned that in many South Asian cultures, the right hand is used for eating and the left hand is considered unclean for this purpose. She also noticed that shoes were left at the entrance, so she made sure to remove hers.

Layla appreciated Alice's efforts and felt that her culture was respected. The two bonded over stories of their own traditions and found similarities and differences that enriched their friendship. This act of cultural competence on Alice's part bridged a gap, allowing both women to connect on a deeper level.

Cultural competence is a sledgehammer that tears down the walls of division. You are culturally competent when you commit to a life of learning, show curiosity about others, and accept the reality that you will never understand the full complexity of all human experiences. The goal is to approach the world with some understanding of culture while allowing people to reveal who they are in each moment.

In this case, the more you acknowledge how much you don't know, the more competent you are. This type of competence is very different from competence in any other skill. Many people commit microaggressions—subtle insults associated with some aspect of identity or culture—because they are incompetent around cultural nuances. They haven't mastered the skill of asking questions that support conscious connections, so they makc assumptions. Usually, those assumptions are incorrect. Often, they're insulting.

By promoting our listening and observation skills, the LOVE system provides a clear path toward cultural competence. Begin by asking questions—the ones in the listening chapter are a great start—then observe people's reactions. This eventually teaches us to sense the mood in any room or interaction, guiding us to make subtle shifts that connect us in more deliberate ways.

We naturally gain cultural competence when we pair that skill with our values—respect, community, family, kindness, or most others I hear in my day-to-day work. Simply put, most don't want to insult others.

Listening allows us to see the walls and observing brings them into focus. Values demolish them.

The CEO whom I met to sign a contract conveyed a set of values through a quick gesture and a request for coffee. However, I am uncertain if these values were genuinely his or merely thoughtless actions that reflect biases or beliefs conflicting with his core values of respect and uplifting people. I suspect that he failed to listen, observe, and live his values, which created a barrier for a conscious connection. Though I cannot be certain of his intentions, I knew I had a choice to protect my self-confidence and regain my power.

I could have allowed his actions to influence my behavior. Instead, I remained aligned with my values. Not only did I solidify this contract, working toward a mission I deeply cared about—I also demonstrated my values by sharing my perspective with him. I value the capacity for people to change. And that conversation demolished the wall he'd built between us that day.

Jim's cultural wall was even more literal. With each presentation, he locked people out—excluding them from the team as well as the room. He hadn't considered that a team member may be late because he's a single father who had to pick up his sick kid from school. He hadn't thought about a team member with mobility issues who struggled to get to the second-floor presentation room. And he hadn't thought about what it might mean to the only woman on his team who, after putting out a proverbial fire with a compromised email server, had to walk to a different building to use the restroom. She showed up two minutes after he'd closed the door.

More than that, he hadn't thought about what the students *in the room* had lost. Perhaps that single father could have enhanced the group's discussion of grit. Maybe the team member with mobility issues would have provided a different perspective on building codes. And maybe the only woman on the team could have shared information about cutting-edge security protocols. Jim hadn't thought about any of that.

In that training, I allowed him to pause and think. He was quiet for a moment—an unusual state for him, at least in my limited experience with him. Finally, he explained, "Punctuality is so important in the military. I started using that policy to demonstrate how critical it is to be on time." I could tell he'd realized the misalignment between his values and the policy and needed to work through the conflict. So, with the goal of pushing him even further, I challenged him. I wanted to show him that the issue wasn't about being a good person or a bad person—he simply brought his own unconscious habits, beliefs, and bias into his work. Most people do.

After a few brief words of encouragement, I asked one more question. "You value service and loyalty, right?"

"Yes, ma'am." His voice regained the confidence he'd started with, and I was grateful for the energy.

"If locking the door prevented people from accessing information that they really needed to do their jobs," I challenged, "would you care more about their ability to work or their punctuality? Which option do you think serves them best? Which option is more likely to result in an employee's loyalty and service to the organization?"

His mouth formed a thin, straight line and he nodded. "Loyalty and service are the most important values of the military," he said. "By comparison, punctuality's pretty low on the list, I guess."

I agree. In the military, punctuality could cost lives. In the training classroom, it won't. Being aware of these differing cultural expectations demonstrates intelligence and competence in understanding and adapting to different settings. This shows the relevance of cultural awareness and adaptation across different circumstances. Do you see the connection?

The point of values is to make decisions aligned with the things we believe to be most important. Often, this leads to sounder decision-making if we pause to consider our *real* goals. Ironically, this alignment often leads us to better outcomes across all things in life and work. We have better relationships, increase the likelihood of promotions, access more opportunities, manage our finances better, and become confident decision-makers.

The walls that exist in the world are made of bricks of vague values and unclear goals. We begin to, intentionally or unintentionally, support a very destructive and painful goal—separation from one another. We disregard values of respect and goals like happiness, joy, and change and create world-changing barriers to working together toward a shared vision.

The most natural human act, connection, allows us to be fully alive. And yet walls persist.

> Cultural competence—including listening, observing, valuing, and engaging—tears down those walls. When we stop merely listing the goals we believe we *should* have, we can strive to align with the values that truly fuel us.

There is a quick strategy to improve cultural competence; I call it the Connection Accelerator Method (CAM). Each week, decide to do something that you normally would not do to expose yourself to different ideas and approaches. Choose a movie that you normally would not choose. Have a conversation with someone that you perceive to be extremely different than you. Ask people about their values. Have fun with this. As you do have these conversations, contemplate these questions:

How are my values and goals different from others?

How are my values and goals the same as others?

How does my behavior change when I am surrounded by differences?

Intensify the exposure to differences and reflect or notice how you are changing and feeling. This reflection can be a small part of your system that connects you with the rest of humanity. It changes you and can change the world.

Make Values Your Muse

Years ago, I was invited to an Esther Hicks presentation. Esther Hicks is a renowned motivational speaker, spiritual teacher, and author who has captivated audiences worldwide. She is best known for cocreating the Law of Attraction franchise with her late husband, Jerry Hicks. Together, they popularized the concept of the Law of Attraction, which posits that individuals can attract positive or negative experiences into their lives through their thoughts, beliefs, and emotions.

At the presentation, Hicks shared something I've thought about almost every day since. "When someone is in my presence," she said, "I want them to leave feeling uplifted or the same. Never diminished in any way."

The moment I heard it, I knew I would incorporate it into my value system. The phrase itself is so simple. And yet, when I think of the profound effect it's had on how I interact with those around me, it doesn't seem simple at all.

I came to many of my value statements in the same way. As I read, watched, or listened to works by people I admire—Bill Gates, Martin Luther King Jr., Oprah, and so many others—I've listened and observed, trying on their wisdom to see whether it suits my core beliefs.

As with the coffee CEO, people tell you a lot about their values if you watch how they act. And thought leaders make this process even easier. We can easily read through their works and watch their presentations, considering what it might feel like to "try on" their values. And when we find one that's a perfect fit, it can become a template for creating affirmations, quotes, and ideas that drive our choices.

Find your muse and, when you have a difficult choice, imagine what a value-driven, world-changing leader might say or do in your shoes. Then, find the courage to make a choice that is different than your first instinct.

Values are an underlying constant; they aren't situational. If we want to change the world, we must align our behaviors with our values—we must act like the person we say we are. We can't call ourselves champions of service and loyalty if we literally lock our teammates out. We can't talk about how much we value equity if we treat others like they're beneath us. Too often we don't realize that our behaviors clash with our intentions. If we aren't listening and observing, we overlook how easily our behaviors are misread by those outside our culture.

When I adopted Hicks's statement as part of my values, I mostly had people I *like* in mind. It's incredibly easy to uplift others when they share your values, background, outlook, and goals. When we encounter those we *don't* like or even people whose views we find disturbing, practicing that value gets a lot more challenging.

I walked toward the front of the room, mind focused on the lecture I was about to deliver to a room full of tenured Harvard professors. Some of my audience, I knew, had appeared on television. Others were bestselling authors. My heart raced with excitement as I ran through my opening lines in my head.

"Excuse me," someone said, interrupting my train of thought.

"Yes?"

"Could you make sure there's toilet paper in the bathroom?"

Time stopped.

I had been so honored to give this talk. In that moment, though, I was that eight-year-old girl again, standing in the restaurant with my dad shouting, "That's it!" Ironically, I was there to give a talk about cultural competence. I was mortified and embarrassed, but instead of reacting, I realized how horrible that professor was going to feel when he realized what he'd done. He'd asked the keynote speaker to change the bathroom tissue!

I immediately knew that I had to replace those opening lines with a discussion of forgiveness. And as I explained the inherent challenges of addressing bias and inequity, I looked at the professor. His face was red, just like the hostess in the restaurant that ignored my dad all those years ago. During the talk, I shared how we recover from microaggressions: we take responsibility for our insults and boldly declare to know better and do better. He approached me after the talk, apologized, and made that declaration. From time to time, I keep up with colleagues and activities happening in the school. He seemed to be active in a long list of diversity and belonging activities throughout the university. I took a deep breath and declared that LOVE won again.

During the talk, I shared how we recover from microaggressions: we take responsibility for our insults and boldly declare to know better and do better.

We adopt values specifically for uncomfortable, unpleasant, painful situations. Those moments—when we feel disrespected or dismissed—are invitations to let our values shine. When we're confronted with someone who is mean, dismissive, and demanding, are we prepared to maintain our values of kindness, care, and patience?

That's the most significant piece about values. When creating this dream world, the challenge is for everyone to identify who they are and who they want to be. Then, we consistently allow our values to choose our reactions, even in the face of displeasure and disappointment.

The LOVE system calls us back to who we really are. By focusing on how our values determine our identities, we reestablish ourselves into more authentic people. That's the whole point of values, isn't it?

Using Values to Close Gaps

"Why did you sign up for this study?" the computer read.

Darius blinked. After filling out the basic demographic questionnaire—height, weight, age, occupation—the moment of truth had arrived.

"I no longer want to feel beholden to nicotine," he typed. With a deep breath, he clicked "Submit." His answer vanished, replaced by a second question and a freshly flashing cursor.

He thought about one form of tobacco or another most days. On the most triumphant days, he conquered the cravings, distracting himself with a long run or a Netflix binge. And yet the clerks at the gas station near his office knew him well enough—he stopped to pick up a pack of cigarettes more often than he liked to admit.

At 43 years old, Darius was fitter than most of the people he worked with. He enjoyed running along a little stretch of highway near his family's suburban ranch-style home and attended a yoga class in a nearby strip mall. A fit, conscientious advocate of outdoor activities, he wasn't the type of person people picture when they think of a smoker. He preferred it that way.

For as long as he could remember, he felt ashamed of the habit. Sometimes he switched to cigars, so he didn't feel like it was *really* smoking. When he got focused on exercise, he'd buy chewing tobacco, telling himself it was healthier for his lungs. The result was always the same—he needed nicotine. And he hated it.

I relate deeply to Darius. For years, I struggled with my weight, resolving every Sunday to start a new workout regimen and diet the following week. Sundays were a day for dreaming, and I'd float through the afternoon, enamored with my vision of a "new me." Armed with a library of self-help books and a cadre of friends cheering me on, I would whisper to myself, "This time, I'm gonna win." I might make it to Tuesday, or I might make it a few weeks. But every single time—like Bill Murray in *Groundhog Day*— I'd wake up one morning to discover that the information, motivation, goals, and strong resolve were just gone. It was as if the goal never existed.

Why do we do this to ourselves?

Why couldn't Darius stop smoking?

Why couldn't Jim see the issues with locking his team members out?

Why did I have the urge to spit in the CEO's coffee?

Why do we behave in ways that clash with our values or goals? That was the exact question a Texas A&M researcher had set out to study.[2] As Darius sat at the computer that day completing his questionnaire, he wasn't really responding to a study about smoking. He was responding to a study about the intention-behavior gap. First applied to patients undergoing physical therapy after a surgery or an accident, the concept of the intention-behavior gap suggests that most patients *want* to change their behavior.

People with serious injuries need to complete their physical therapy regimen—and most know that. If they fail to complete their exercises, the result is often a lifetime of pain and discomfort. The same was true for Darius's smoking. As he moved through the study, he learned that he succumbed to his addiction primarily in three key situations: when he drank with friends who smoked, when he experienced higher-than-average stress levels, and when his sleep was disrupted. In short, he failed when life got in the way.

We can refer to these triggers as habits, autopilot, or zombie behavior—regardless of the term we choose, the result is the same. When we allow ourselves to become unconscious, numb to the world around us, our old habitual behaviors lurch forward, independent of the dream we have for our life.

Listening, observation, and values work together to reveal the gaps between our intentions and our behaviors. Even more important, they replace our old habits with new ones. That's how I lost weight and made peace with my body. It's how smokers quit tobacco. It's how the coffee CEO shifted how he treated me and others. It's one thing Jim, Oprah, Bill Gates, and Esther Hicks have in common. They all reached their goals by consciously and intentionally recommitting to the work of a value or principle-based life every single morning. In the case of Hicks, she practices the art of allowing things to flow—thinking thoughts that raise our energy and feelings of goodness—but the result is the same.

Moving toward cultural competence requires you to examine your intention-behavior gaps when connecting with other cultures. Challenge yourself to evaluate the wisdom and truth in your behaviors from an outside perspective. Commit to increasing knowledge about how you intend to treat others and how you actually treat them. And train your inner voice to stop making excuses—have the courage to see the misalignment in your behaviors, and if you truly care about living your best life, shift back to places where you feel free and connected.

That's not the only way cultural competence leads you to your best life. When you learn and work to interact with compassion and empathy toward others, you also learn to extend that empathy and understanding to yourself. In the same way you learned to listen to and observe others, cultural competence helps you extend those values to yourself without limits, bias, and judgments. That's the key to decreasing the gap between our intentions and our behaviors. It is all about comprehensive LOVE for self and others.

By changing ourselves—by digging deep down and committing to live our values—we can change the world. Give the gift of your values by practicing them every day. Through that one simple practice, our LOVE can spread like a shockwave, uplifting everything and everyone it touches. It becomes a salve for our families, our communities, our organizations, and the earth itself.

Be that shockwave. Live your values and then share that value with the world.

It turns out Darius's perspective helped researchers better understand the intention-behavior gap. The Texas-based study found that to truly align our values and behaviors, we must clarify our values, believe them, and associate them with our identities. Allow your values and who you want to be (your evolving identity) to drive your choices. Then, your life will move in the direction of the things you really want. You can tap into the power of unlimited possibilities.

What Are You Worth?

Jared rubbed his eyes and sighed. Slumped in the chair across from me, he ran his hand over his tightly cropped hair. His shoulders were wider than most men his height, but at that moment, his navy-blue striped polo shirt looked much too large. Like a child wearing his father's clothes, he looked exaggeratedly small and somehow afraid. He looked up at me, dark bags under his eyes and hopelessness in his posture.

Even after 11 years in prison, Jared had risen to the role of vice president of his company. He knew he'd been lucky—a March 2018 Brookings report found that nearly half of all returning citizens (people who have been incarcerated) weren't able to find a job for at least a year after their release.[3] His friend had gotten him an interview at her company, and, after 10 years of determination and diligence, he'd turned that entry-level job into an executive role.

Jared's workers loved him. In his role as vice president, he'd managed dozens of projects and designed several new brand initiatives. He'd taken leadership trainings and excelled at motivating his team. During the decade he was with the company, he'd become one of their most beloved employees, well-liked and respected by those above and below him in the corporate hierarchy. And then the company was sold. Jared's department was cut.

As a bit of severance, his CEO gifted him a few coaching sessions with me. Our task was to find a path forward for him, transforming the disappointment of a failed company into new opportunities for growth. Given his exceptional leadership training and background in corporate management, it should have been a piece of cake. I saw the coaching as an opportunity to help Jared identify his passions, goals, and interests. With his background, he could have done anything—so there was a good chance that losing his job was a blessing in disguise. In our first meeting, I told him that.

He laughed a little, and I saw a shimmer in his eyes. "I don't know about that; this job was a miracle given my record," he said, his voice softer than I'd anticipated.

I smiled at him—the warmest expression I could muster—and nodded. "I know that this is a big change for you. Let's take this one step at a time," I told him. "Let's play with possibilities for the moment. I need you to make a list of everything you could do. Don't filter yourself—just list all the possible jobs you could see yourself in."

When he came back the next week, he handed me his list. "Jobs I could apply for," he'd written at the top. Below that, he listed the following:

- Convenience store clerk
- Night janitor at an office park
- Plumber's apprentice
- Uber driver (sign-on bonus?)
- Fast-food worker
- Hotel night auditor
- Salesperson (Steve's Discount Furniture?)
- Landscape maintenance person
- HVAC salesperson
- Truck driver
- Painting crew

- Warehouse worker
- Highway construction worker

I read through the list, interested in the options he wrote down. While I had not anticipated his list exactly, it didn't surprise me. Not really. Even though he'd been a successful executive at a major company, I saw something else operating in him. I understood what was driving his choices—identity.

Identity Shifting: Break Your Limits

All the jobs Jared listed add enormous value to our society. Who would want to work in an office park that didn't employ a janitor? How disappointed would our children be if there were no workers to prepare their Happy Meals? And if I had to paint my own house, the result would be disastrous!

And yet many people find Jared's choices perplexing. I didn't. Several years ago, I did a day-long workshop for the Pivot program at Georgetown, a program that encouraged returning citizens to tap back into their power and bounce back after decades in prison. Like Jared, they needed to restore their values and rediscover their ability to prosper despite limitations. The challenge was believing that options and possibilities were truly limitless.

Others wonder why an executive would choose to apply for entry-level positions. With little sense of who he *really* was and how he saw the world, they struggle to make sense of his choices. Jared used to describe himself as a felon—it was part of his identity—but becoming an executive changed all that. It had replaced his identity as a felon. So why had he listed jobs that were so out of alignment with that evolved identity? With his newly found values? Where had the executive in him gone?

I thought I knew. I'll bet you do, too, if you really think about it. It seems that his identity was contingent upon keeping the job as an executive. Still, I wanted to find out for sure with an exercise I call "identity shifting." Here is how it works:

I asked Jared to think of someone else, someone he admired and respected. "If you had to name someone who absolutely radiated success," I asked, "who would it be?"

He tilted his head back and stared at the ceiling for a few moments. When he looked up, he had a grin on his face. "Harvey," he replied, "from *Suits*."

For those unfamiliar, the character is a corporate attorney known for his ability to close nearly any deal. He's beyond confident, flashing high-end sports cars and well-fitted designer suits. Despite a list of struggles and value conflicts that make his character interesting, Harvey is a charming, sexy character whose over-the-top charisma makes him irresistible—both on the show and for viewers at home.

Harvey's high-power status aligned well with Jared's experience, so I responded with enthusiasm. "I love it!"

He seemed pleased, until I pushed him just a bit farther.

"Now," I said, leveling with him. "Forget about yourself. What would Harvey do if he were in your exact situation?"

"Oh!" he shrugged, his eyes sparkling in a way I hadn't seen before. "I mean . . . he'd probably start his own thing," he said, straightening his back. "Hang out in five-star hotels to meet people, maybe."

I nodded, encouraging him to go on.

"Well, but first, he'd start talking to people. He'd go into that Rolodex and call everybody he knew." He'd been slumped down in the chair just a few seconds before. With an energetic adjustment, he leaned forward, his elbow on his knees. He smirked, adding, "And he'd start pulling in favors."

I grinned and tilted my head. "Huh," I said. "So those are things Harvey could do? But you couldn't?"

Now it was his turn to tilt his head. Realizing what I was getting at, he stopped in his tracks, and a big, charismatic grin spread across his face. He didn't even protest.

Jared allowed his perceived identity to distort reality and limit his choices. Yes, his struggles have some truth, but the alternatives he allowed himself to explore did not have to fit into the box of "what kinds of jobs might ex-offenders be able to land." He needed to create his own opportunities.

Jared was missing a crucial point—aligning his intention, values, and behavior with his desired identity. He limited his potential by solely identifying as an ex-offender. Although he recognized the significance of this alignment, his past experiences often overshadowed his current accomplishments, making him feel restricted. Yet, he got the point. Jared utilized the technique of "identity shifting" to remind himself that valuing his journey and aligning with his core values allows for an abundance of choices, despite any setbacks.

We come across our identities honestly. What I mean by that is that the stories about our lives are filled with both facts and fiction. When screenwriters, like the one who created Harvey, develop characters, they do so by creating experiences and circumstances that match the character.

There's good money in truck driving and our world couldn't function without good drivers. Besides being one of the most dangerous jobs in America, it requires a high degree of training and responsibility. But never in a million years would anyone suggest that Harvey become a truck driver.

When I was struggling with my weight, I observed something interesting. I always wanted to be the down-to-earth characters in movies who ate the burger. The women who ate salads and low-calorie foods were often characterized by sharp attitudes and rigid existences. In the end, although she is typically skinny in movies, the character that is more relaxed gets the guy. So I prided myself on eating burgers, hoping to have my cake and stay trim. These choices began to feel in contradiction to my value of health and energy. Although I do not desire perfection, I try to implement the phrase I coined, "identity shifting," to help me reach my goals. To shift my identity and achieve better alignment, I say things like this to myself: *I am the kind of girl that eats healthfully most of the time. I am a meditator that goes to the gym and can also sit back and have my cake now and then.*

We are who we think we are. On a practical level, this means that we must change our thoughts about ourselves to get different results. So, I had to create a character that aligns with the image of my best self. This is why we call it a self-image. How do you imagine or see yourself?

Harvey's value lies in his ability to overcome obstacles and use his power to create circumstances that reflect that power. While there's plenty of value in driving trucks—or working at a fast-food restaurant or a warehouse—those jobs would not have aligned well with Harvey's skills. They wouldn't have aligned with Jared's skills either.

Until he learned to shift his identity to a more expanded view of himself and let go of the fear, he couldn't see it. Valuing yourself may mean breaking the limits of old identities.

What's on Your Card?

Pick a card—any card—and write on that card a few words describing who you are.

This is a prompt for one of my favorite exercises that I ask participants in corporate training to do in class. Many write things like "Sales Manager," "MBA," or "Supervisor." And while all these descriptions are perfectly reasonable, accurate descriptions, they don't come close to approaching the *secret* words all of us have on our cards.

I learned my secret description years ago from my mother. She woke up at the crack of dawn each day to drive me to a private school that was two hours away.

A chubby kid with long braids, I spent a lot of time complaining. I had to eat peanut-butter-and-jelly sandwiches for lunch when I would have rather had turkey and cheese. We had to drive an older car when other kids climbed into their parents' shiny new sedans. And I didn't get to go on the shopping sprees I imagined other little girls indulged in on the weekends.

One day, as I wound up to start my regular complaint-packed ride to school, my mom stopped me. "Talia," she said, her voice quick and sharp.

Oh no, I thought. I went too far.

Instead of yelling at me, though, she knelt, so we were eye to eye, resting her hands on my shoulders. She looked first over her left shoulder, then her right, scoping out the nearby areas as if she were on the lookout for spies. Leaning in, she whispered, "I wasn't supposed to tell you this. . . ."

Eyes wide, I gasped, "Tell me what?!"

She shook her head almost imperceptibly and spoke again, this time even quieter than before. "I wasn't supposed to tell you until your 18th birthday. . . ."

Overwhelmed with curiosity, I leaned in close to her and blurted, "What is it?!"

A few seconds passed as she looked behind her again, just to be certain that no one was listening. "If I tell you this," she said with the solemn, measured tone of an FBI agent, "you have to promise not to mention it to anyone in the whole world. I have been sworn to secrecy."

Moving swiftly from wonder to concern, I choked out a quick, "I-I promise, Mom."

She nodded, resolutely. Then, in a voice too quiet for me to hear, she whispered something.

"What?!" I asked.

"You are a princess," she repeated, her voice so quiet I had to strain to hear her.

This stopped me dead in my tracks. Searching my memory for some joke or family reference, I came up blank. So, as uncertain as I had been before, I again asked, "What?"

Conspiratorially, she continued, "You're a princess, Talia. And this is your test of humility—it's to teach you to be humble, kind, and helpful."

I just stared at her, trying to process what I was hearing.

"Remember who you are, Talia. But do not tell anyone."

I nodded. "Okay . . ."

Just before she stood to usher me into the car, she said one more thing that has stuck with me since that day. "Show them who you are through your goodness."

My heart dropped. Although I was shocked, I told her that I'd suspected as much. There was nothing in me that day that doubted for one moment what she said. Sure, there were lots of questions to be asked and details to be sorted out. In retrospect, I'm grateful that I had no interest in what was real or true. Being told I was a princess just felt good, and it changed my entire experience.

I walked into school the very next day with perfect posture, confidence, and a bit of a royal wave as my morning greeting. I stood up for the bullied, I picked up trash in the halls, I stopped looking for others' approval, and rather than feeling bad about my PB&Js, I started offering to share them with others in exchange for their lowly turkey and cheese. Most of all, I stopped complaining about the things I didn't have.

It felt great to matter. It felt great to walk around with the knowledge that my identity and my story had meaning.

My circumstances did not mean that I was less than the other students. On the contrary, my struggles were an initiation—a series of challenges meant to test my grace. In this way, I transformed my doubt into confidence and my dissatisfaction into patience. I learned to accept what I had and released the insatiable desire to be validated by others. After all, I was a princess.

The seed sown by this "secret" followed me into my adulthood, even as I grew out of the literal belief in my personal royalty. A litmus test, this framework helped me to make decisions based on the choices any princess-turned-queen would make in the face of adversity and uncertainty. It was that seed that helped me go to college with virtually no money and thrive. It was that seed that helped me graduate from grad school at the top of my class with a newborn baby. It was that seed that helped me start my own business. Inspire others. Write this book. And it's that seed that keeps the fun in my journey as a single mom who forgives and accepts that everyone has a rite of passage in the life of royalty.

As a child, I wrote something false on my symbolic card—something that framed me as less than. Something that limited my potential more fully than any outside force could. I share this story every time I teach this lesson. I encourage people to take their card and tear it up. Create a new description. I still do this exercise for myself today. My new card has written, in bold, green letters, the words "Goodness Creator."

And so I say to you: Find your inner princess, or prince, or king, or queen. Stop feeling like an impostor and embrace the vision of yourself that you can admire. What that vision consists of is entirely up to you. Your success is whatever story you want to make up and whatever triumph makes you feel like your journey is meaningful. Consider defining success on your own terms, without fear of judgment or criticism. Consider defining success without having to answer why or defend the realism of your ideas. Consider defining success without the need to defend your identity. Value yourself, and the rest will follow.

To LOVE Is to Uplift

One of my core values is empathy—I strive to uplift and understand people.

I uplift people even when someone tells me to get them coffee.

I uplift people when I see them being rude to others.

I uplift people when they seem sad and dejected.

And I uplift people when they're in the middle of chaos.

Most of the time, it's not easy.

And I am far from perfect. Like everyone else, I get attitudes and forget about my own LOVE system. So I uplift myself when I make mistakes and offend people.

Living out our core values requires us to do two things at once. First, we must do the challenging, introspective work of understanding our true values. Through this process, we become more self-aware, uncover the assumptions and judgments we tend to make, and take a front-row seat to our deepest motivations and intentions. Values mold our perceptions of the world and others, undergirding everything we do, say, and even think. Although our values can transform over the course of a lifetime, our core values remain relatively stable. They're the core defining concepts of who we are.

For many people, figuring out their values illuminates so many things. They realize why they feel unsatisfied in their new job, why a recent venture felt like a disaster despite reasonable profits, or why a friend of a friend makes us feel uncomfortable every time we see them.

While identifying our values is transformative and important, most people already realize this step is needed.

The second step, on the other hand, often eludes us.

The way we communicate our values, both verbally and through our actions, strongly influences how others feel in our presence. This is a crucial aspect of taking responsibility for the power we wield in every interaction. People who feel valued are more motivated and make fewer mistakes. The most productive institutions and cultures are ones that cultivate a sense of respect, integrity, and appreciation for good work. Even when results don't meet expectations, management theory indicates that emphasizing the value of workers' contributions rather than criticizing their failed attempts is more likely to lead to improvements.

As leaders, we're responsible for articulating and honoring behaviors that reflect our most deeply held values. Implementing your core values in life and work may sometimes mean rethinking other important values. After all, life is about choices. Intentional choices are the surest way to live our values.

Align Values, Change Company Culture

Dear Talia,

We spoke at one of your presentations six months ago, and since then, I haven't been able to stop thinking about some of the things you said. Then—and now—we keep losing talent. It doesn't seem to matter how hard I work to retain people; we always lose our best employees to competing firms.

My leadership team is all on board with your message. I consulted with them about small changes we can make. And, together, we decided to add a ping-pong table to the break room. I've started paying for company-wide lunches on Fridays. I've even approved additional vacation days across the board.

Nothing seems to help.

After I saw you speak, I recommitted to living my values—honesty, efficiency, and learning. My team is on board, too.

So why can't I get my employees to commit?

Sincerely,

Frustrated CEO

When responding to a letter like this, I'd start by saying something that reflects good listening and observation habits:

I'm so glad you've made the switch to run your organization life with LOVE. I am glad that your team is on board. And I can sense your disappointment and frustration with losing talent.

Don't stop now!

When you honor organizational values, it will help create a more positive culture and a more profitable company. The team's buy-in is critical because the LOVE system isn't something you can "tweak" once a year at an administrative retreat and expect a culture shift. It becomes a part of the way you operate. You listen to each other, observe connections and feedback loops, revisit and align your key priorities with your values, and you engage the entire organization.

Across your organization, everyone must turn these habits into competencies—people must be clear on what LOVE looks like in your company. Living your company values may have become part of your leadership approach, but until it becomes truly system-wide, there will still be zombies lurking within your company. Once those values—and the behaviors that reinforce them—have trickled through your entire company, the culture shifts will blow your mind.

Probably seems impossible right? Is 100 percent buy-in in a company a possibility?

Elevate the goal and see the results.

Not only is that level of participation possible—making conscious connections part of our daily habit ends up being the most natural thing that any of us could do. Once we live our values daily and live with LOVE in all aspects of our lives, the world around us begins to shift. We literally feel better, live happier, and see our values spread beyond ourselves into every corner of life.

Your employees need to learn that aligning their priorities with the organization's values is not a checklist or a chore to be done. It is a daily choice to listen, observe, value, and engage. It is your leadership's responsibility to train employees to increase capacity to listen, observe, and operationalize values. Then, LOVE habits get integrated into the organizational culture. Creating the values was just the start; even modeling them within your office or in a board meeting is not enough. Authentic connections are dynamic— they need to be nurtured, grown, and practiced. Stay on the path.

When my company performs organizational culture assessments for clients, we begin by listening—from breakrooms to boardrooms—to gather perspectives as a part of our systems thinking approach. We've seen a lot of breakrooms with ping-pong tables and arcade games, but those aren't the things we are looking for.

We look to see whether people at all levels can articulate how company-wide behavior aligns with company culture. Because if we want to shift company values, the process must involve everyone. And if we want to see wins in areas like retention and recruitment, we need to train the entire organization to have a shared model of what this looks like. If we value respect, does that look like a smile, kind words, acknowledging everyone's contributions? Typically, respect is shown through effective communication skills.

Zombies thrive among others like them—those that feel comfortable on autopilot, those that are happy not changing or not connecting, and those who are not living with LOVE. Essentially, the zombies are people who don't listen, don't pay attention to others, are self-centered about their needs and values, and are poor communicators. Before you start scanning your office and labeling others as zombies, start with reflecting on your own zombie moments.

In an organization of any substantial size, the zombies will seek each other out and take comfort in their shared inaction. If zombies are allowed to continue, this "go along" approach will work to undermine LOVE at every turn.

The good news is that a few zombies lurking isn't always a bad thing. They can represent an important feedback loop in the system. Zombies will challenge you to find ways to hold everyone accountable for living core values. And test the strength of your efforts. Zombies typically wake up and turn into learners who end up thriving in cultures that are persistent about operationalizing their values.

But, I've got some bad news: zombies like to play ping-pong, too.

Culture shifts need to happen at a much deeper level than simply adding additional employee perks. The changes this CEO is seeking require a shift, so I'd suggest one in this situation.

The next time you're confronted with any challenge or obstacle, gather the data that listening, observing, valuing, and engaging provide you. Keep trying new things and observe the results. When you feel discouraged, create a "go-to shift" to remain in a mental and emotional position to impact change.

Here is a shift for this frustrated CEO and others frustrated with results. This shift will help you think about the situation differently to increase your energy and mood in order to gain clarity about your next strategic steps:

I am so grateful that I have built this amazing company. I'm really excited about what I am learning. I am learning from both my successes and challenges. I want to do a good job here. When people leave, it makes me feel uncertain. I feel good about how much I care about people. I know that I want to build a company where people want to stay and grow. I am looking forward to figuring this out. I am excited about listening to my people and uncovering ways to make this company the best place to work!

I am looking forward to getting clear. I might play ping-pong with the team and chat about the culture. I don't need to have all the answers today. I am very resourceful, and life has allowed me to connect with smart people who have found creative ways to address retention.

I'm going to sit down with a cup of tea. I will get quiet as I connect with my intentions to grow this amazing company and take good care of the people who are continuing to help us grow. What is the most important decision I need to make in this moment? How can I be more efficient? What can I learn from this experience? What stories or lessons can guide me here?

It's tough to create strategies and keep people happy—there are a lot of things going on in the world—but I know that if I keep making decisions based on data from LOVE and a sincere desire to serve, I will create the desired outcomes. I feel excited and humbled by the limitless options available. This challenge is a wonderful opportunity for me to make an impact.

This may be an opportunity to better clarify my company's values. This could be an opportunity to listen to those that have left and better understand what drives and motivates people.

Can you relate to the frustrated CEO? Are you feeling frustrated by the lack of results in your company or life? Don't worry, you are not alone. It's natural to feel let down when you put in your best effort and fail to see the desired outcome. Don't lose hope. Add resourcefulness to your list of values to enhance empowerment and confidence, then the right actions and answers will naturally flow to you. When we listen, observe, and align with our values, we expand possibilities. If you need more guidance or feel stuck about your next move, read *Decisive* by Dan and Chip Heath. The authors provide strategies to overcome emotional bias and make more confident decisions. By incorporating these strategies into the LOVE system, you can align with your values and expand your possibilities, ultimately leading to more meaningful and effective actions. It's easy to judge things superficially, taking a narrow and shortsighted view. But taking a step back and asking, "Is there more to this story?" is crucial to seeing the big picture and avoiding hasty judgments. To do this, you have to stay attuned to values, yours and others, and continue to make a conscious connection to what matters most to you.

Recently, I saw an experience play out in my backyard. At some point, a hawk moved into the area behind my house. A big, beautiful bird that dominated the sky. There I was, enjoying my coffee, listening to the birds, absorbed in the LOVE experience, and in flies this huge, imposing bird. I just observed.

Every day, this hawk returned until it became a part of my morning— it joined my system. Then it wasn't *just* the hawk that I observed; the other smaller birds continued to scatter and peacefully fly in spaces close to the hawk. I thought, "Oh, how scary for those poor little birds." Early in the morning, I would witness the hawk dive and eat a smaller bird. It made me wonder why all the birds didn't fly away faster when the hawk came near. Indeed, there was enough space to fly somewhere and live outside this hawk's threat. I was baffled. Although I understand the circle of life, I was a bit sad for those birds. Curious to learn more, I researched hawks.

As it turns out, hawks play a significant role in controlling the population of prey animals in their respective ecosystems. For example, a decrease in the hawk population could lead to an increase in prey animals, causing overgrazing and damage to vegetation. This is because prey animals, when overpopulated, can have a devastating impact on the ecosystem. By feeding on these animals, hawks help maintain a balance in the ecosystem and prevent overpopulation. Additionally, other animals in the ecosystem behave differently around hawks. For example, small birds may take cover or scatter when hawks are around. In some cases, hawks may cause other animals to move to different areas of the ecosystem, which affects the vegetation and habitat.

It is important to maintain a balance among different species to ensure the proper functioning of the ecosystem. The hawk actually *improves* the bird population. Without the hawk there to cull the smallest and weakest of the birds, the ecosystem would be thrown out of balance. A study, published in *Nature Ecology & Evolution*, examined the effects of raptor declines on ecosystems across the globe.[4] When there are less hawks cascading, it leads to the extinction of some species.

That hawk is like the frustrated CEO's perception of failure. He was concerned that losing employees reflects poorly on *his company* and *that his efforts to fix it did not work.* This might be a very limited view of the situation.

Losing people to competing firms or any other observation that seems "bad"—like that hawk—might be an important part of the system that drives improvement.

Identify the natural systems and rules that drive people in your organization. What needs to happen to bring balance and stability? People and businesses are studied as much as science and nature. Some of the most fascinating innovations in our world are based on observing nature. This process is called biomimicry—a term that refers to humans' tendency to build things that reflect nature's successes. Armadillo backpacks, for example, or trains with the shape of a bird's beak.

These innovations came about by studying the animal world. Over time, we find that there are constants that we can rely on. There are also surprises and changing environmental conditions that alter the impact of our choices. In a business, changes such as social justice issues, politics, technology, population changes, resources, and competition challenge us to observe and experiment with our systems and structures.

So, what are your constants? The LOVE system is designed to help you fully capitalize on core skills that will inform how you manage everything else. What are core things that make a difference in the system of human motivation?

Human desires and core values are closely interconnected, as the combination of underlying desires gives rise to our core values. These four underlying desires are control, security, belonging, and a sense of purpose. The pursuit of these desires is what shapes our beliefs, attitudes, and behaviors.

For example, the desire for control motivates individuals to seek success and achievement, while also driving perfectionism. The desire for security encourages individuals to seek stability in their lives, such as financial stability or job security. The need for belonging drives individuals to create meaningful connections with others and to be part of a community. And the desire for a sense of purpose motivates individuals to create meaning in their lives and make a positive impact in the world.

The combination of these desires can lead to a paradoxical situation— people desire to be unique yet be a part of a group or team. This need to belong yet retain individuality often results in individuals seeking groups that align with their core values. They want to be accepted for who they are, while contributing to something bigger than themselves.

Thus understanding these underlying desires and core values is essential to understanding human behavior and motivation. By acknowledging these desires, we can begin to understand why individuals behave the way they do and what drives them.

As we evolve, at our core, we want to be aligned with our values (or do what we think matters). We want to be happy. We want to like our job. We want to love our lives.

Most humans want the same things. The answer to making everyone happy, healthy, and well-adjusted doesn't lie in ping-pong tables or a free lunch—although I suggest companies that offer these perks continue to do so. It lies in thinking of your company as a system—and seeking help from others to understand what's going wrong *and* to identify what is going right to uncover underlying needs, desires, and values.

Whatever it is, the most important thing you can do is maintain consistency. Even when you might not have a clear connection to your vision and values, trust the LOVE system. If you can hold to these daily habits, you'll feel like a raptor—with keen eyesight and the superhuman ability to see how the world works. Before you know it, you'll know exactly how to soar in your company and within your life. And then you can change everything.

What a fantastic world we can create together—all of us on the journey to live our values and wake up from the nightmare. We can jump out of bed, connect with those still in zombie mode, and free us all. All it takes is the daily strategic practice of true LOVE. All those connections we form. All of that strengthening of our system. To LOVE is to practice four habits until they become a part of who we are and how we behave in the world. Imagine feeling connected and at peace as you generously give and receive gifts of wisdom and talent, without even thinking about it.

LOVE is a daily practice. For it to be effective, we must make LOVE a habit that we engage in daily.

Plant Value Seeds and Nourish the World

Each of us wakes up in the morning with a new slate of opportunities. As a new day dawns, we can once again choose what we value most. We sometimes get it wrong, like Jim, Jared, and Darius. We struggle with distractions, sometimes forgetting the value we bring to the world. Other times, we lose sight of others' unique contributions. So how do we know whether we've achieved what we set out to do? How do we weigh a larger salary with a more compelling organizational mission? When do we choose our own needs over the demands of family life?

As a new day dawns, we can once again choose what we value most.

Effective leadership demands that we strive for clarity, but that clarity won't always come easy. It requires a daily recommitment to being intentional—about what we value, how we act, and what those actions mean for others. We can embrace our homes, workplaces, and neighborhoods, not just as spaces —we can break free of the zombie urges and use these venues to articulate what's most important to us. Oprah has been doing this for decades. Jim needed to make a few tweaks, but I heard he always leaves his meeting room doors open now. Jared embraced the opportunity to realign his identity with his values. And, by the way, he's currently enjoying life as a millionaire. And the frustrated CEO continued to align with his values, implemented a creative recruitment process, rotated employee positions instead of focusing on retention, and has won awards in the region for being one of the best employers.

Living by values is like planting seeds. You can sow the seeds of your beliefs with every action you take, and in time, they will take root and flourish. You must nurture and care for them daily, providing water and attention until the seedlings become strong and robust. Like a gardener planting a garden, by aligning your behaviors and values, you can help create a better world for everyone. Are you interested in growing with me and planting the seeds for a values-driven world?

Take a deep breath. What is important to you today? Can you listen to your thoughts and words? Do your behaviors and choices align with your values? Can you create a new character based on a new vision of the world?

TAKEAWAYS

In this chapter, we've learned the importance of studying our core values and consciously acting on those values.

In the LOVE system, the word "value" includes how our values determine what we do and the value we place on ourselves and others. The word also means *worth*. Do not be confused by semantics; this part of the system is about exploring what matters most. Everything that we do, all that we are, and the earth itself share a desire to be valued and connected. Values drive your choices, and your choices create your reality. After reading this book, I hope you add conscious connections to your list of core values.

> *The leadership skill enhanced by aligning values is cultural competence.*
> *The parts of life most impacted by value alignment*
> *are happiness and well-being.*

Below are key ideas to take with you:

- **Study your values.** What are the most important values to you? Can you stay aligned with your values despite circumstances? Understand your values and practice using them to drive choices.

- **Everyone must contribute.** This means we all must contribute to practicing LOVE in our daily lives. We inspire others to join by having discussions about what value-based habits look like in action.

- **Live your values.** Perhaps the most impactful piece to remember, living your values means exhibiting behaviors that align with your core values. This alignment of belief and action is what creates who we are and drives results in life. Without action, values are meaningless.

- **Build cultural competence.** Moving toward cultural competence not only means recognizing differences but also adapting our behavior to build more conscious connections. Find ways to listen and value people from all backgrounds. Encourage others to share their stories so they feel valued. We want to adjust our attitudes and behavior to help us shift from judgment to curiosity.

- **Evaluate your evolving identity.** Don't let your character limit you. What's on your identity card? Review how you describe yourself and assess whether this description maximizes or limits your potential to make a difference in the world.

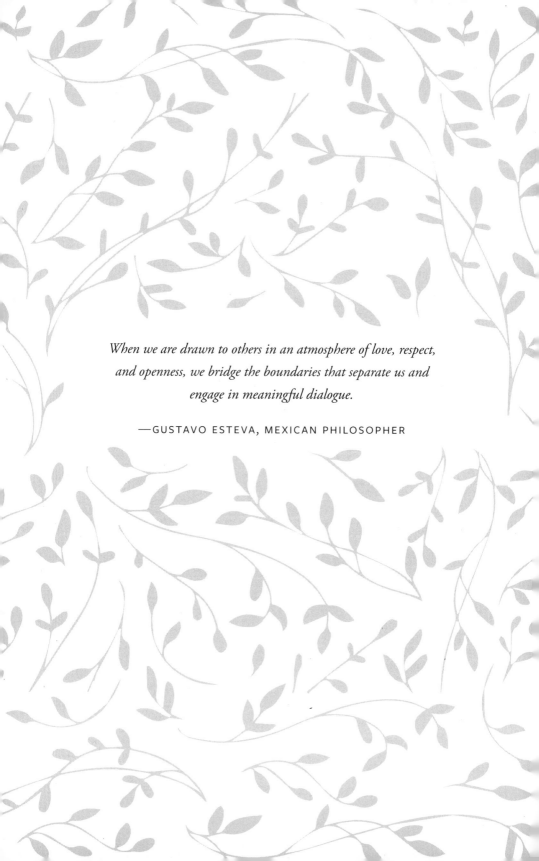

When we are drawn to others in an atmosphere of love, respect, and openness, we bridge the boundaries that separate us and engage in meaningful dialogue.

—GUSTAVO ESTEVA, MEXICAN PHILOSOPHER

CHAPTER FIVE

ENGAGE

———

Better Engagement, Better Results

When you master the tools in this book, you will sound more competent and professional than 90 percent of the people around you. I've landed jobs for people who were 60 years old, who thought they were too close to retirement to get a job. I've helped people nail interviews after nine months of rejection. Alonzo was both.

I sat him down and talked him through listening, observing, and values, and he went out and nabbed the first job he applied for.

He was back in my office just a few months later.

Compared to how he'd looked before we started working together, he looked like a polished, joyful version of himself—but he still wasn't happy.

"So, what's going on, Alonzo?" I asked. "You were so happy to have this job!"

He shook his head and rolled his eyes. "Whenever I pop into my CEO's office, he cuts me off. Sometimes, he tells me he doesn't have time for me—that I should reschedule with his secretary." He rolled his eyes again at that, and I nodded. People give you a lot of information in their body language if you just observe them. "He'll cut me off sometimes or hurry me along. Then, the other day, he literally made a phone call during our meeting. I was talking, and he just picked up his phone, dialed it, then asked if I could come back later."

This process is about feeling strong, professional, and empowered.

He looked at me as though he expected a sympathetic response. Before I share what I told him, let me say that treating any other human being this way is not only poor leadership, but also mean and rude. The challenge is that if I focus on the boss's behavior with Alonzo, I am allowing him to shrivel into a powerless victim. And this process is about feeling strong, professional, and empowered. So, instead, I asked, "Well, what things are you talking to him about that are important to him?"

"What do you mean?" he said, his eyes wide.

"How much time did you spend thinking about what matters to your boss when you decided to take up his time?"

This apparently wasn't the response he'd expected. He sat for a moment in silence.

"Did you give any thought to what you'd talk about with him? Did you think about what would matter to him?"

Finally, he replied, "Well, no. There are a lot of things I need to know about."

"Is it rude that he cuts you off," I asked abruptly, "or is it rude that you don't take the time to figure out what's important to him?"

He stared at me, stunned, but I could almost hear my point land.

This was going to be an easy case. I gave him my advice and sent him on his way, instructing him to schedule with my assistant in a few weeks.

He was on the right path.

He needed to double down on his listening skills and practice using systems thinking by observing feedback loops. Then he needed to understand his boss's values.

He needed to engage to be more conscious of and connected to the goal.

He needed to engage to be more conscious of and connected to the goal.

Do you think that you could create a shift for Alonzo or identify how his thoughts and behaviors are contributing to his frustration? Let's make a few connections to themes covered in this book and learn more about the final habit, *engage*, before addressing Alonzo's issue.

You can apply the art of shifting to absolutely any situation. First, you change your perspective by using language connected to values. Then, you *engage* in thinking that shifts your thoughts toward new possibilities. These kinds of shifts in thoughts and behaviors quiet the zombified inner voices and instantly give you an identity makeover. In the nightmare, our thoughts are familiar and on repeat. We forget to change the track. Sam Cooke plays indefinitely. The shift takes a familiar thought

Change your perspective by using language connected to values. Then, you *engage* in thinking that shifts your thoughts toward new possibilities.

and gives it a new song. When you deliberately create new ideas and perspectives, you operate based on new beliefs. As a result, you enjoy a completely different experience without needing any circumstances to change.

In so many ways, Alonzo reminded me of Cole, who I met at the "Art of the Shift" event. When Cole rambled on about his boss's feedback, I listened with purpose. I wanted to get inside his mind, to understand what made him tick. I observed, too. In his slumped posture, the way his suit hung on his body, and the way he grunted his responses, I saw the same loneliness, depression, and isolation I see often. And I asked Cole about his values. With his short, three-word response, I helped him shift his problem into a set of statements designed to realign his behavior and perception of his circumstances with his values.

The shift we have learned so far is about engaging with our own thoughts. Changing your thoughts can instantly pop you out of a nightmare and pave a road leading to bliss. Yet most of us need help. Our brains are subject to negativity bias—a tendency to favor the negative view of things. Or it can seem like we are addicted to certain ways of telling our stories. Cole likely talked about his boss and the pain surrounding his experience to so many people that he convinced himself that he was a trapped victim.

It reminds me of how the circus trains large elephants. As calves, they are tied to a post unable to escape. At first, they try. Then they grow weak. Eventually they forget that escaping was ever a goal. Once they transform into massive, strong creatures with the power to break any barrier, they no longer try. They have learned to be helpless. They stay tied to that post when all it would take is a gentle kick to free themselves from bondage. If these elephants could talk, they would need help realizing that their perception of what is real is wrong. The shift is your gentle kick. Engagement is acting on your escape plan.

The E in LOVE (listen, observe, value, engage) is all about how we engage with others to experience the power of conscious connections. You need to listen, observe, and align values to effectively engage with purpose.

We cannot leverage the power of our connections with others and reconnect to our common purpose if we cannot sustain attention. We need to both engage and be engaging. Engaging communication should be considered a sport. Winning means that we have achieved the purpose of the interaction. Common reasons that we communicate or engage others is to teach, inform, motivate, express feelings, or meet some social expectation. Being aware of your purpose makes you a conscious communicator. Using this awareness to engage will help you feel and be more connected.

Do you ever wonder why magicians never reveal their secrets? The reason is simple. The sleight of hand that makes the trick work isn't where the magic lies. The magic lies in how the trick makes us *feel*.

That evening on stage with Cole, I used one simple tool to draw out people's deepest happiness within seconds of meeting them. I didn't use sleight of hand—no rabbits in hats or disappearing pennies. Nothing I did that night was a trick. It was a strategy that involved listening, observing, valuing, and engaging. I used my daily, committed practice of this book's tools and added just a hint of magic to keep my thoughts organized. The magic is in the rules of engagement.

The Rules of Engagement

Our brains remember things that come in threes. If you grew up before cell phones, you know this instinctively. Think back to your childhood best friend. What was their phone number? If you're like most people, you can remember the first three digits—the area code—and the second three digits. Those last *four numbers* elude you. If only telephone numbers came in three groups of three.

Conscious connections are about being aware of humanity's interdependence. We understand what it means to live together in this world, and we are conscious about how our choices impact our interactions with people. This process is both existential and practical. It is a system of ideas about the meaning of life and practical habits that result in a better collective experience. We can become prescriptive in our approach if we lean on researchers who have cracked the code. We have some intel about what engages the human mind. Marketers know to what and how long we will pay attention. Social media platforms and tech giants have discovered how to make scrolling and apps addictive. We can leverage these often controversial approaches to create power and transform how we live and lead change.

The term "rules of engagement" comes from military directives. It directs military forces to know where, when, how, and with whom you can act against. Words, crafted well, are powerful tools that can be used to solve big problems. The rules of engagement are designed to urge you to be more aware of how you communicate with others and increase the likelihood of more productive interactions. These rules can be applied to every type of engagement. From everyday conversations with someone on an airplane to a speech accepting the promotion of a lifetime. If you can commit this outline to memory and use it to organize your thoughts and world, you will master a habit that will transform how you live and lead, especially in a world that is riddled with distraction and, consequently, disconnected.

1. Have a clear purpose or goal when you speak. (For casual conversations, it is okay for learning and connection to be the primary or only goal. If this is the case, you may not need the next two steps. You can engage with a clean slate.)

2. Preselect three core ideas that will help you achieve your purpose.

3. Drive your purpose home.

That's it. Short, sweet, and easy to remember.

While most people think that better communication means *longer* communication, that viewpoint couldn't be further from the truth. Time is our most valuable resource in this fast-paced, overloaded, overwhelming, zombie world. And the only way to engage is to get to the point. That's what I told Alonzo.

Whether or not his CEO's behavior was rude, I knew one thing for sure—Alonzo's behavior of popping in to ask a busy executive a million disconnected questions was rude too. He needed to improve his communication strategy if he wanted to turn the relationship around.

"Make an appointment with him for a one-on-one," I told him. "When you get to that meeting, ask one simple question: 'What's important to you?' Then just listen. Observe when your boss lights up, when he gets excited, and what he spends the most time talking about. When he's finished, thank him, and leave the meeting."

With that, I sent Alonzo off with everything he needed to pull a rabbit out of a hat.

Ask Better Questions

The quality of your questions in a conversation easily measures the quality of your listening. The quality of your leadership is measured by the questions you *ask*, not the questions you *answer.*

This is the most powerful tool you can implement in your personal and professional life. The power of questions is seen in famous speeches, where they rhetorically serve to suggest or allude to great unsolved problems— and neat and immediate solutions do not necessarily follow them. This is why they are called thought-provoking questions—they are intended to encourage, inspire, and invite listeners to greater levels of thinking and imagination. These questions move the listener beyond mundane, day-to-day matters to big-picture issues, motivations, values, and long-term goals. The answers aren't the point. The questions themselves reframe the goal. The questions extend our reach toward that next mark on the wall.

The purpose is to make sure that our behaviors align with our values and goals, things that are serving you and the rest of the world well. We need to be present, and we need to be alive and open for that to happen. By asking the right questions, we place ourselves in the seat of engagement. And engagement opens us up to new possibilities and outcomes in life. When you have a problem to solve, instead of searching for answers, create a list of questions or goals. That's what I told Alonzo to do.

After he left my office that day, he did exactly as I asked, returning with a clear sense of his boss's values and priorities. We brainstormed a script he could take with him to his next meeting. Just like in English 101, we sketched out the following outline using the rules of engagement:

- **Purpose:** Update. Prioritize. Clarify. Remember the purpose of the conversation!

- **Introduction:** I just need 15 minutes to share an update, prioritize goals, and clarify expectations.

- **Point 1:** Update about productivity in research and innovation.

- **Point 2:** Question regarding the alignment of budget and priorities.

- **Point 3:** Clarification of expectations for the quarterly report.

- **Conclusion:** Thank you for your time. Can we follow up with another 15 minute check in next Tuesday after our two o'clock meeting to close the loop on these things?

To get Alonzo that job, I'd been his cheat sheet. I'd been a surrogate for him, tracking down the company's values, telling him what to listen for, and coaching him in his observations. Once he got the job, though, he had to do those things on his own. He had to be the one to engage others. We needed to explore these three questions:

1. What do I do with the wisdom of listening, observing, and aligning with values?

2. How do I and others benefit from the power of my daily LOVE practice?

3. How do I engage in conscious connections that get results?

It's the same thing I did back in Detroit that night—how I engaged thousands of people simply by stepping into Cole's problems. It's the same approach I use to turn 10,000 hours of leadership guidance into four habits. It's an everyday tool you can apply to life, work, and world challenges. And it was the same way I taught Alonzo to finally impress his CEO. The answer also comes in a group of three.

1. Engage your thoughts to gain a new perspective.

2. Engage others with clear communication and quality questions.

3. Engage others in choices and ideas that elevate the goal.

Show Me the Money: Elevate the Goal

What if I asked you to earn $100 by the end of the week? There's only one catch—the money can't be your own. Really. Think about it. What kinds of things would you do? Would you ask your mom? Dig out that Instant Pot you got for Christmas three years ago and post it in an online marketplace? Maybe you'd call five friends and ask each for 20 dollars. Or apply for a credit card. You could probably brainstorm several more options, all of which would be easy, even in that short period of time.

Now, could you come up with $100,000 by the end of the month?

Stop for a moment and think about it. If you really needed a hundred grand within 30 days, what would you do? No cheating—don't look ahead for the answers. And remember, your task is simply to generate a list of ideas. You don't need to determine whether they would work.

When you finish your list, it probably looks a lot different from your previous one. Some people consider business ideas—consulting work, renting their home or car, or taking on a few side jobs. If you're lucky enough to have a rich uncle, you might give him a call. You could take a second mortgage on your home. Max out all your credit cards.

Suddenly, your list of options would have one thing in common: bigger.

What changed? The answer is simple—the goal. When the goal changed—literally increasing, in this case—you instinctively reframed your thinking. You tap into greater possibilities.

This challenge can also reveal something about your values. If you decide to ask your parents for money, you may value community support. If you choose to sell things from your garage, you demonstrate resourcefulness. And if you max out your credit cards rather than borrowing from people you know, you may be signaling your investment in independence. Reflect on how your values drive your decisions. How can you use your values to reach for larger goals? Engage in experiences that elevate the goal and stretch your mind!

The capacity to stretch our limits often unveils new possibilities. This notion brings to mind a common exercise I've observed in corporate training sessions, an exercise that serves as a vivid illustration of this concept.

The room falls quiet as the facilitator speaks. "I want you to stand in the center of the floor and reach for that distant object toward the wall," they say, pointing toward the far end of the room. "Even if it seems impossible, try to touch the wall."

The participants nod and begin to reach, stretching their arms out as far as they can. But they soon realize that no matter how hard they try, the wall remains out of reach. The object in the distance mocks them, and soon they are forced to give up in defeat.

But then, the facilitator returns with a twist. "Try again," they say, a slight smirk on their face. "It's actually easy."

The participants are taken aback by this new instruction. They hesitate for a moment before slowly reaching out again. But something has changed—they feel a newfound sense of determination, an energy that permeates through the room.

And then the impossible becomes possible. Those who previously couldn't even get close to the wall can now touch it with ease. The object in the distance is now within reach, and the participants are exhilarated.

This exercise demonstrates a powerful truth about human behavior: We are often limited only by our beliefs and perceptions. When expectations are placed on us, we tend to live up to them, even if they seem impossible at first. But when those expectations are shifted, and we are presented with new instructions, we can break through those limitations and achieve more than we ever thought possible.

> By shifting those expectations and pushing beyond our perceived limitations, we can achieve greatness and make the impossible possible.

So the next time you're facing a seemingly insurmountable challenge, remember this exercise. Remember that expectations, and the beliefs that follow them, have a profound impact on our behavior. By shifting expectations and pushing beyond our perceived limitations, we can achieve greatness and make the impossible possible.

The idea of setting "stretch" goals is well-known, but it's often underestimated, especially when facing tough challenges. Tony's story provides a perfect example of this.

Tony found himself in a financial storm, burdened by a massive $350,000 in debt. He was living on credit, using it to pay his monthly expenses. He felt beaten and overwhelmed.

In response, Tony began to plan for survival. "I might have to live on peanut butter and jelly sandwiches for a while," he thought, "and cancel my gym membership. Maybe even limit time with friends. I'm in over my head, and I can't see a way out."

But then, things began to change. With a bit of help and kind words, Tony started to reconsider his situation. I asked him, "What's most important to you, Tony?"

He responded immediately, "Health, happiness, and my relationships." I then shared a piece of advice that had helped me during tough times.

"Tony, making tough choices is hard. It's normal to feel embarrassed or ashamed. But remember, you deserve a good life, today and every day. It's okay. You're going to be okay. Don't be afraid to stretch yourself. Believe that life can be better."

I suggested Tony think about new ways to increase his income. "What financial goal would make your current debt seem small?" I asked. Inspired, Tony set a monetary target that would dwarf his current debt and started outlining steps to reach it.

Eighteen months later, Tony had transformed. He was healthier than ever, having prioritized exercise and healthy eating. He had started a business with friends, and it was more successful than they could have imagined. His once overwhelming debt was now just his mortgage and car loan.

The power of stretching your limits can be liberating! Take a moment and think about the possibilities. It's strange how people often predict negative outcomes but dismiss positive ones as unrealistic. Both are just predictions, but they inspire very different actions. Negativity can hold you back, but thinking about limitless possibilities can lift you up.

Consider reaching beyond your current problems, aiming for a goal that at first might seem out of reach. Tony's story is proof of this power.

We can make stretching beyond limits a team sport. Engaging others in questions that challenge the mind and test limits is a simple way to tap into the power of a conscious connection (a connection designed to achieve limitless possibilities). Finding creative ways to engage with each other is the secret to turning teams, communities, societies, and countries into innovative powerhouses. Do you see the power in this simple exercise? Starting with small, bite-size goals can be motivating and help you keep the momentum. But who is responsible for changing the target, elevating the dream, and creating the big vision? *You*, perhaps? Typically, it is the person that is patiently listening, quietly observing, making connections to core values, and creating a plan to engage the masses.

LOVE is about you harnessing your power to engage with the world— your family, your community, and your work. We cannot live our values without engaging with our environment. We listen to give, we observe so we can do better, and we consider our values to live and share them. LOVE spreads when we engage.

One Engaging Question

Pam was snarling. Again.

I was teaching a class on interpersonal skills and asked participants to pair up for a communication exercise. They rose from their seats and scanned the room for their perfect partner. Pam crossed her arms across her chest and, with a scowl that rearranged her entire face, spat out a question we'd all heard from her before: "Why?"

A woman across the room rolled her eyes. Shaking their heads, two more made eye contact across the room. "Surrender to the process and just do it," I said, expecting and embracing resistance.

The class had been going on like this for several days. Pam always had something to say, whether it was a snarky little comment or a rude, dismissive question. The rest of the participants learned to see it coming. Completely disengaged, she kept her distance from everyone else in the class. She seemed to prefer it that way.

Even without talking to her, I knew something else was going on. I first suspected she'd picked up her mannerisms from someone in her family. Maybe her mother tended to criticize her. Maybe her grandmother always made that signature snarl. Like the rest of the class, I believed her behavior was part of her personality. Or did she just have poor engagement habits?

So, I pulled her aside during a break. After all, nobody else was going to. As we chatted over chips and salsa, I realized I'd never seen her up close. Her face looked drawn and tired. It was clear that her life wore heavy on her shoulders.

"So, Pam," I started, after taking a sip of my water. "Can I ask you something?"

"Sure," she replied, her face devoid of her typical scowl.

"What's important to you?"

That one simple question unlocked her spirit, opening up her authentic self. As her story poured out, I learned she had a son with special needs and an aging parent who needed around-the-clock care. She juggled her work and family responsibilities the best she could. Then an upcoming merger forced her to be reassigned to a different position in her company; now she had a much longer commute. She was overwhelmed with the changes that came along with her new position. The cost of caregiving had already carved a deep hole in her retirement fund. And, amid everything else in her life, she had to make time to attend this training.

As she spoke, her voice grew warmer. Her eyes, although tired, sparkled when she told me about how much she cherished the time with her mother. With a gesture of enthusiasm, she told me about her son's speech therapy progress. Her body came alive, and I finally saw *her*. Not her snarl or her scowl. Not her snarky comments. Not her disengaged behavior. *Her*.

> That's the power of quality engagement. When we are conscious about the complexity of our shared human experiences, always remembering that everyone has a back story, we create space for *real* connection.

Questions give us a perfect opportunity to engage. If we really listen to the answers and observe mannerisms, we get clues about the other person's values. From a single question—What's important to you?—I learned a lot. While I enjoyed hearing about her family and her life outside the class, that wasn't what made the biggest impression on me. The most important thing I learned that day was that Pam was utterly, unapologetically, shockingly fake. She came across as a harsh and rude person when her acts of kindness were beyond count.

Engage to Reveal Your Authentic Self

Most people wouldn't describe Pam as *fake*. Usually, people use that term to mean someone who is over-the-top friendly—someone who laughs and shallowly asks about your family. While she did none of those things, she shared one thing in common with people like that: her behaviors didn't reflect her authentic self.

Pam was one of the most loving, kind people I've ever met. As we talked, she told me about her family and things she was concerned about. Thanking me for inviting her to lunch, she told me, "People always think I'm mean and standoffish." She flashed a sheepish grin, slid out of the booth, and hoisted her purse over her shoulder. "I have no idea why."

She had no idea why.

Reader, I mean it when I tell you that it could not have been more obvious if it were written in black marker across her forehead. From how she communicated to how she scrunched up her face—the choices of words she used and how she used those words—every behavior I saw in that class was off-putting.

"I guess it's just how I am," she said with a shrug.

"Would you like to learn some strategies to change that?" I said, careful not to offend her. "You're so kind, giving, and compassionate—and I wonder if I could share some things to help you align yourself with who you really are. What do you think?"

A couple of weeks later, we met again and went through her communication choices. We started with body language. Then we moved to her habit of cutting people off and speaking over them.

"You have such a giving nature," I told her. "And none of those behaviors reflect that."

She became more open to the experience and decided to change what she could. After a few weeks of listening, observing, and considering her values, we put her on a feedback diet. She would spend 90 days asking questions of the people she interacted with most. By asking, "How do

I come across?" or "What are some things you've observed about how I communicate?," she was arming herself with enough information to truly evaluate her barriers to engagement and connection.

When I saw her next, she was a different person. She was bright and cheery—always smiling. She had an entirely different way about her. "It's weird," she said. "I didn't understand what you meant when you talked about feeling more authentic. But I really do! I'm so much happier. I'm so much more . . . me!"

Through that process, Pam learned something important: Engaging questions are the shortcut to authentic living. We become the most authentic versions of ourselves by zeroing in on our values and recognizing how those values align or don't align with our interactions with others. Most of us simply slide by on the types of interpersonal interactions we were raised with. We imitate our parents, friends, aunts, and uncles. And then we call that behavior our "personality" or our "authentic selves."

> How often do you question the thoughts you hold about yourself? *Just because you think it does not mean it is true.* And just because you behave in familiar ways does not always mean that you are being your best self.

Consider how you behave and interact with others. Do you have relationships that work? Are you being true to your values and ideals? Communication or engagement habits, like the ones Pam displayed at a workplace training, were not a part of her personality. Instead, these habits were likely related to how she responded to her anxiety of life.

According to the Anxiety and Depression Association of America (ADAA), more than 40 million adults in the United States alone deal with anxiety—that's 18 percent of the population.[1] Chronic anxiety is a big problem that requires strong support. If you feel anxious, you are not alone.

There are things you can do to manage anxiety more effectively. Taking an existential approach might be a helpful option to pair with your daily practice of LOVE. This approach urges you to see anxiety, or even anguish, over the past or present circumstances as an opportunity for more authentic living. In other words, embrace the opportunity to "get real" and engage in honest self-reflection and conversations with others. You will gain insight into your values and beliefs and learn to use signals of anxiety as a reminder to live in alignment with your principles and values. With help, Pam was not only able to recognize how she was dealing with her anxiety about life and work, but she was also able to accept her freedom to make choices.

Ultimately, going on a feedback diet and getting coaching enabled Pam to be mindful of the connection between her actions, relationships with others, and building a happy and meaningful life.

Essentially, when we have no playbook on how to move forward in life or we feel completely unsure of how things will turn out, we get anxious. At the same time, most of us understand that we have control over our behavior, and we are clear that different choices will indeed lead to different outcomes. It just feels like a lot of pressure! Pam wasn't completely oblivious about her behavior. After all, she was mandated to attend an interpersonal effectiveness training. Yet she needed to make more conscious connections by engaging differently and owning her freedom to choose. "We are capable of actively influencing our thoughts, feelings, and actions. Until we accept our capacity for freedom, we will not change."[2]

Engage in a journey of self-discovery to become more truthful, widen your perspectives, and explore what gives meaning to your life. Pam needed a path forward. Our LOVE system uncovers connections between what we are experiencing in the world and how the world is experiencing us. We do not run from anxiety and pain; we face it with confidence knowing that every connection is an opportunity for growth and expansion. Until we learn to implement the LOVE system, we're all doomed to living out our lives, engaging in hollow choices that do not fulfill us, honor our values, or integrate us into our communities. What a lonely existence that must be. And, on top of that, you feel anxious and fake.

We do not run from anxiety and pain; we face it with confidence knowing that every connection is an opportunity for growth and expansion.

Million-Dollar Leaders

Imagine being on a reality TV show, divided into two teams, each with a leader who's responsible for leading the team to victory. You and your team must come up with ideas to make one million dollars. Despite being two steps ahead with a list of possibilities, the red team's leader assigns a strategy without asking for the team's input. Meanwhile, the blue team's leader prepares their team with thought-provoking questions, such as "How can we leverage our collective skills and encourage innovative and creative thinking?" The blue team's leader sparks a list of ideas, and team members begin to collaborate and buy into the task.

Consider the power of the leader who maps the following eight questions:

1. How can we leverage our collective skills?

2. Can we brainstorm ideas without judgment? What are the possibilities?

3. How do we encourage innovative and creative thinking?

4. Have we considered everyone's values?

5. What are you willing to do to reach this goal?

6. What are you not willing to do?

7. Can we do anything to make this task easy and honor our values?

8. Is there something we think is hard, but would be easy if we were fearless?

Leaders who understand the power of provocative inquiry unleash their team's greatest potential and creativity. By encouraging big thinking and innovative solutions, it primes them for success. In contrast, those who assign a strategy without input lack buy-in, reducing the chance to win. As Jim Collins says, "Ask the right questions."

Therefore, great leaders make rich connections by being great listeners and curious observers, honing their humility, and inspiring action. They are responsible for developing effective systems that engage both the head and the heart. With the right mindset and the right questions in place, there's no limit to the potential of an engaged team.

Engage to Build Health and Community

The largely unremarkable town of Roseto, Pennsylvania, has a population of 1,567. Meaning "rose garden" in Italian, the small town was founded in 1882 by immigrants from Roseto Valfortore who came to America looking for work in nearby mines. With brick-lined streets and limestone buildings, the town is speckled with quaint reminders of the town's history. Sadly, those reminders are dwindling. So is the average life expectancy of Roseto's citizens. So, when Joseph sat down to talk with researchers about his lifestyle, he was surprised by their questions.

"What kind of car do you drive, Joseph?" the woman asked.

"Car?" Joseph responded curiously. "I thought we were here to talk about my heart."

The woman nodded. "Indulge me."

For the next 30 minutes, Joseph talked about cars. He didn't really mind. A car lover all his life, he could have spent hours talking about his favorite makes and models. Joseph was proud of his BMW, and he told the interviewer so. "I decided to go with the Gran Coupe xDrive since it came with the turbo engine and all-wheel drive," he boasted. "Not that I do anything crazy with it, but it's nice to show off a little power every now and then."

Joseph was surprised by the interviewer's question. And yet she knew exactly what she was doing. Twenty-five years earlier, nobody in Roseto would have talked about "showing off" personal possessions. In the early 1960s, Roseto was a town steeped in the traditions on which it was founded 75 years before. Little had changed by then; the children, grandchildren, and great-grandchildren of those first Italian Americans held firm to their community. It made sense. They'd all but fled to Roseto to escape the bigotry their fellow immigrants faced at the time. They wanted to build a paradise. And they succeeded.

Fueled by their traditional Italian heritage, the "old ways" persisted into the 1960s and 1970s. The family—not the individual—was the town's primary unit of measurement. Among all Rosetans, the community provided a solid foundation. Residents felt a deep and sincere responsibility to protect and nurture it. Households often contained multiple generations, families were readily prepared to celebrate the smallest victory within the community, and the elderly, rather than retiring to nursing homes, were elevated to a kind of "supreme court" in the town.

We know all this because Drs. Bruhn and Wolf conducted an in-depth study of Roseto in 1962.[3] They chose the little town because Roseto had the lowest occurrence of heart disease in the area. While neighboring towns were similar in terms of lifestyle choices, socioeconomic makeup, forms of stress, and levels of success—with many towns even sharing the same water source—Roseto's residents stood out as remarkably healthier.

If anything, the researchers mused, the Italian American community—with its penchant for fried meatballs, high-fat diets, and hearty wine and cigar consumption—should have *led* the nation in heart disease. But that wasn't what the numbers showed. Bruhn and Wolf theorized that the community itself supported the health of those within it. The community increased their heart health, happiness, and general well-being through daily engagement.

The family unit was the "smallest" unit of membership back then. Instead of one sibling going to a birthday party, the entire family attended. Instead of one parent visiting someone sick in the hospital, everyone went. Community events were universally attended. Social events *became* community events. And with that heightened social connectivity came heightened support for one another and the community. Love spread between community members like a network of connection and care. And it propped everyone up, not just emotionally—but physically as well.

"Do a lot of people like to show off their cars?" the interviewer continued.

"Well, sure, some may try," Joseph bragged. "I've got most of them beat. I may not have the *best* car in the neighborhood, but it's not far off."

By the time researchers spoke with Joseph in 1985, much had changed about Roseto. The phonebook, at least, looked nearly identical.

While tradition played a deep and personal role in 1960s Roseto, the commitment to community declined sharply by the mid-eighties. In the 1960s, the community firmly believed that "showing off," displaying wealth, and even doing too much to look good, bred jealousy, resentment, and bad luck—they thought it could bring the wrath of the "evil eye." The belief goes back hundreds of years in Italy, and it came with those early immigrants to America.

"Why are you even asking me about my car?" Joseph asked, exasperated. "So what if I like to show it off?"

It would be silly to think that driving a fancy car alone is detrimental to your health. Yet, if the intention behind owning the car is to create jealousy or set you apart from others—in other words, to disconnect you from your community—maybe it's not so silly after all! The belief in the evil eye was just one of a handful of beliefs that researchers studied when they went back to Roseto 25 years later. They also looked at other traditions—other markers of community—as well as the town's overall views on family and community. When researchers studied the town in the '60s, they had an inkling of what was coming. As the original study concluded, researchers made a bold prediction. They predicted that if the belief in the community faltered, the rate of heart disease would increase, matching that of Roseto's neighbors. They were right. The community weakened and so did the hearts of its inhabitants. As larger homes replaced modest ones, as interest in community centers waned, and as people broke into smaller, more isolated cliques, Roseto transformed into any other town. Their natural approach to engagement disappeared, replacing residents, one by one, with zombies.

There is so much power in the way we build communities and engage others, but I am also aware that engagement can be hard. For some, known as social butterflies or extroverts, connecting feels energizing and fun. For others, including more introverted people, engaging feels like it drains them and disrupts their peace.

Some share that they strive to disengage as much as possible. And, honestly, given all the hard things happening in the world in life, I don't blame them. Some tell me that they don't *want* to engage. Some people even say they don't want to be bothered with talking to others—especially people they don't know.

"What do you think people misunderstand about you?" a colleague asked me. She was shocked at my answer: "I am an extreme introvert and feel energized only when I have huge chunks of time alone." My work, life, and this book are about conscious connections, so this answer surprises people.

Practicing the LOVE system gives me clarity about how to prepare for engagement. When I study my needs and take good care of myself, I do it in the service of others. Here we see the leadership paradox: *It is all about you and not about you at all.* I selflessly care for my needs and sometimes selfishly engage to reap the benefits and power that conscious connections provide.

Could it be a coincidence that I have never met a disengaged person who seems genuinely healthy, vibrant, and happy? In my line of work, I have had the chance to dig deeper. Like Pam, most are dealing with insecurity and some form of anxiety. Without support, the people with "engagement" hang-ups passionately defend their choices.

So what if I ignore people?

So what if people think I'm scowling?

So what if I avoid my boss because I don't like her style?

It's just how I am.

Most defend their choices with rigid insistence that disconnecting from the world is a better path. Yet each person that I have ever challenged on these choices seems to keep listening; they keep coming back. They stay and fight until they wake up and connect again. Ironically, these clients are the ones I had to use the word "hard stop" to let them know that our session can't run over. They are thirsty for engagement and connection. And I am happy to embark on the journey out of zombieland with them. I know I need gentle reminders to stay aligned with my intentions, too. We all do.

That's the thing about engagement. We can't engage alone.

Just like the citizens of Roseto needed each other, *we* need each other. Mastering the art of engagement can feel like magic in a world of zombies. And it is, in a way. Engagement is the final and most important step in the LOVE system—it's the one consistent action that brings everything together. It's the most powerful tool in a toolkit full of world-changing strategies. It's also a tool that relies on others. Engagement demands that we reach out to those around us and bring them into our circle.

I'm certain Pam didn't enjoy asking others for feedback on her demeanor. Like all of us, she must have been uncomfortable hearing others' responses to how she looked and acted. Pam realized what so many others miss—it doesn't matter how *we* think we're engaging. What matters is the connection we make with others. How we impact others boomerangs right back to our hearts.

No Time to Engage? The Fast 15!

Dear Talia,

I've committed to leaving zombieland behind. As you suggest, I wake up every morning and commit to the LOVE system, and it's done wonders for my work life.

With my two teenagers' eyes glued to their phones, sometimes my home feels like ground zero in the zombie wars. I come home from a full day of work with no energy to fight with them about their devices. And when I make them put their phones away, they just grumble and sulk—not exactly a recipe for engagement.

Am I fighting a losing battle?

Sincerely,

Zombie Dad

As a mom, I feel Zombie Dad's struggle! The good news is that he *isn't* fighting a losing battle—but he may be forgetting that the LOVE system requires us to be open to others. We need to demonstrate competence in teenage culture. Even when we have the best intentions, forcing our perspective on others—our children included—will never lead to conscious connections.

This situation, like any other, demands that we step back, observe what's really happening, listen to others and ourselves, and reflect on how our behaviors communicate (or don't communicate!) our values.

Zombies are easy to spot when they're on their phones—but technology isn't the only way to spot a zombie. When we expect our kids—or our spouses, coworkers, and friends—to go through the motions of what we *think* engagement should look like, we're recreating the nightmare. That kind of interaction isn't a true connection, no matter how great it looks from the outside.

Instead, the dream requires us to look inside, listen to ourselves, and observe how our interactions work—and how they don't. My advice to Zombie Dad would be to, first, step back. Ask yourself how you're engaging with your kids. Are you meeting them at their level? Do you invite them to talk about the things that are interesting to them? Have you put in the effort to learn about their interests without having an opinion about them?

If not, start there—we are responsible for bringing our most engaging selves to the people we care about. Until we do that, it's hard to blame our kids for choosing texting or social media over their parents' boring questions!

Once you've really listened and observed—and not a second before—try implementing what I call the Fast 15.

My youngest son knows that engagement is important to me, but he reminds me from time to time that he has his own hopes, dreams, and preferences—so, sometimes, he brings his phone to the dinner table. As human beings with lives of their own, teenagers have the same kinds of stress, pressure, fatigue, and desire that adults have—and they've learned that their phones are an easy outlet for satisfying those needs. Sometimes, they just don't want to engage outwardly.

And here's a secret: sometimes *I* don't really want to talk to *him* either! Particularly after a hard day—and especially when we're trying to (re) commit to LOVE, it can be tempting to try to force him to put his phone down. I stop myself. Remember, the LOVE system asks us to live our values.

One of my values is freedom of choice—it's important to me that my kids grow up with some level of independence. I want them to practice making their own decisions. That means I have to carry that value to the dinner table, no matter how tired I am, no matter how annoyed I am with the phone use, and no matter what I anticipated for quality engagement. I still strive to honor my values.

Sometimes when we get annoyed with our kids, our impulse is to snap at them. We want to judge them for being addicted to technology or video games; we take their actions very personally. We want to shout, "Why are you resisting my attempt at being a great parent? You know how important it is for us to engage?!"

Approaching things that way—even when we intend to bring LOVE into our homes—only leads us back to zombieland. We discover quickly that our true intention is to feel good about our parenting skills, not necessarily to really connect. Instead of observing opportunities to connect with another kind being, we look at *their* behavior as barriers to our own personal vision and goals. It's a quick fix—a move that may address the symptoms in the moment but will always fail to get to the root issue.

After you've yelled at your kids, after they've surrendered to your requests, what happens then? They jam their phones in their pockets, then push their food around their plates, silently shutting you out. Or they shovel dinner into their mouths as fast as they can, then ask to be excused.

Maybe you get a few shallow answers in between quick, messy bites.

"How was school?"

"Fine."

In the end, all we've done is annoy them.

And my guess is, by the end of that conversation, you're annoyed, too.

This is exactly the type of situation LOVE is designed to address. The system is a way for us to connect deeply—consciously—with others. It goes well beyond the symptoms of disconnection, pushing us past the typical Band-Aid fixes we read about on social media or parenting blogs.

What if, instead, you shifted your perspective? By repeating the following out loud, you'll be amazed at how much your outlook changes:

I'm so happy for this opportunity to sit around the table with my children. Even in our busy lives, we are finding time to be together. I value love and engagement, so I want to cherish our time together. Part of loving my kids is allowing them the freedom to discover their own values; this includes connecting with the people and entertainment they choose. I want to love them by setting appropriate boundaries. I can find a balanced and productive way to achieve that. I can also love them by giving them the freedom to choose. This can be easier than it seems. I love being in the flow. What if I invited them to work through the LOVE system with me? What if I took a break from forcing things and discovered what really matters to each of us? I bet it would be fun to create a solution that allows us to form conscious connections because everyone is happy and free to participate—and we all commit to valuing and loving one another in the best ways we can. It might be fun to have a LOVE chart instead of a chore chart for a while.

This challenge is very real for me. My teenage son is a musician. He loves his headphones and is constantly creating music. He is consciously connected to music.

One evening, as we sat down to eat, he had ear pods in one ear. I was getting angry, but decided to eat in silence until I could calm my mind, shift, and begin to reflect on how I could connect with and respect him. Did his disconnection make me feel disappointed? Frustrated? Lonely? Sure! I really value my time with him, and I was hoping to connect with him. My older son was off at college, and some nights it was just my younger son and me sitting at a table that could fit 10 people.

I didn't put any of those feelings on him—instead, I invited him into a conversation.

"Hey, let's talk for two minutes, I'll put the timer on and then you can go back to your music. By the way, I am really excited to hear your new music," I said. "I value us connecting, and I know we don't seem to have that much time together. Any ideas about how we can spend a little more time together, without taking away your sense of freedom?"

Together, we came up with the Fast 15—a tool we still use today. We literally set a 15-minute timer. (I do this for all kinds of things—it makes cleaning the kitchen feel like a breeze!) During that time, we all have to stay engaged—myself included. And after those 15 minutes of total focus, everyone can scatter. Fifteen minutes is the perfect amount of time. No matter how tired we are, we can focus for 15 minutes. And, yet, it's long enough to allow us to truly connect.

The best part about the Fast 15 is that, sometimes, the timer goes off—but we're all feeling so energized by our time together that we don't want to stop. Without the timer, it seems that we lose focus and let our phones turn us into squirrels. With a small, shared commitment—just 15 minutes—we've found that we can pick each other up, often erasing some of the stress of the day through our conscious connections. Some people will object to this approach. They worry about involving their kids in this kind of decision—after all, they're teenagers. What if they simply choose to keep their phones out?

This objection isn't rooted in LOVE. LOVE requires us to listen to others, to observe how we interact, and to *live our values.* Whatever your values are, I'll bet they don't include forcing your children to do things they don't want to do just to make yourself feel better. And that raises an important point: The core of this question isn't about phones. The core of this question is about *connection.*

All kinds of things get in the way of connection—we see that every single day as we make our way to and from work. Simply curbing distractions doesn't automatically create connection. We need the LOVE system for that. We must consciously commit to nurturing our relationships in a way that honors each other's values. We have to listen, observe, value, and engage consistently. When we get too focused on the details and forget to observe the systems at play, we miss our opportunities for connection.

The effective fix—stepping back and observing our family systems—takes a lot less work. It is a more pleasant way to see how beautiful our world is. When we look at our family dynamic as a system—and acknowledge our role in shaping that system for better and for worse—we trigger the domino effect of behaviors that nurture the healthy, loving relationships we all crave.

We can show our kids how to create those relationships for themselves.

No matter how difficult it may seem to change our everyday behaviors, feeling disconnected is hard. We have the opportunity today to help our kids and others in the world find fulfillment and build a value-based future.

By practicing these skills—namely, bringing others into problem-solving conversations, observing the smaller systems of our lives, and setting ground rules that align with group values—we develop skills that translate into other aspects of our lives.

The Fast 15 is a simple tool you can use in the workplace, with friends, or at your dinner table. I promise that the process of engaging with skill and structure will translate into results beyond measure. When you find yourself in a department meeting where everyone seems buried in their laptops, you'll know how to come together, talk through the challenges, and set healthy ground rules to make the workplace more fulfilling. If you have a night out with friends but find that one of them can't stop complaining about their ex, you'll have experience helping everyone communicate their needs and finding a common ground to make sure everyone in the group feels heard. And those random team meetings where everyone seems to have their own agenda and you can't seem to get anything done? You'll be well-prepared to lead a conversation about the group's goals as well as the basic parameters that keep the group functioning in harmony. You need 15 minutes to drive change.

In all cases, you'll find *yourself* better able to connect. Often, we believe technology or a long list of other things is the problem when these distractions are only a symptom of much larger issues. When we come together to listen, observe, communicate our values, and truly engage, we inevitably find the distractions melt away. We simply don't need them anymore.

In real time, when we're staring at our teenagers across the dining table, furious at how oblivious they are to the family, it is much harder to see opportunities to improve anything. We can quickly adopt the wrong approach, "solving" a zombie scenario with another equally unhealthy nightmare.

With a lot of practice—and a lot of LOVE—we begin to see our solutions ripple out like waves in a lake. Seemingly small solutions, like the Fast 15, impact far more than our dinner-table conversations. They help our children develop healthy connections. They increase our capacity to lead and set an example for everyone we meet. LOVE really can change the world, even when the problem seems as mundane as getting our teenagers to share at the dinner table. All it takes is a conscious effort to connect with those we love. Wouldn't it be funny if a 15-minute timer was the thing that changed the world?!

Life Is Short: How Will You Spend Your Time and Energy?

Imagine your life when you finish this book. As your eyes flutter open, you jump out of bed and greet the world. You make a commitment to LOVE, actively choosing to approach the day with purposeful listening, careful observation, and behavior that aligns with your values. You grab your lunch and travel mug and head out your front door. And all you see are zombies.

How do you engage a zombie?

Believe it or not, you've already taken a decisive first step toward engagement. You were present enough to sense the mood around you. You were engaged enough to observe others' detachment. And you held to your values even when those around you failed to demonstrate theirs.

The final component of LOVE's magic, engagement, is the key to effective leadership, stronger relationships, and a healthier society. It's deeper than that. Without engagement, how do we know we're even alive?

When I think about authentic engagement, I remember the feeling of touching my infant son's tiny toes. I remember finally hearing the word *mama* among his sweet little babbles. As I watched my boys grow, I held tight to their sweet smell and the wonder that shone in their eyes. When my children were little, I felt like I loved them *too* much. Now that they're older, I realize they don't remember much of it. But I do.

That kind of engagement—using your values to purposefully listen and observe—seems natural when we think of it in terms of parent-child relationships. When we interact with babies, we don't expect anything in return. We just offer ourselves—all of ourselves—to nurture, love, and uplift them.

When we bring that same level of investment to everything we do, regardless of what we get in return, we know that we've truly mastered engagement. We've done something worthwhile in this limited time we have on this earth. And whether others recognize our efforts or not—fair warning, zombies rarely do—we've made the world a better place.

After teaching thousands of classes over the years, I began to see connections and themes. All problems—technical, emotional, social, political, and cultural—are rooted in the absence of LOVE. When spouses argue, they've usually failed to listen. When companies fail, they've inevitably observed the wrong metrics. Traditional organizations often fail to engage, and start-ups typically forget to identify their deeper values. People who are unhappy with their jobs often need to listen to their own hearts. Other times, they find that they're observing with too much judgment. Money issues, addiction problems, loneliness, depression, and fear all can be solved by strategically thinking about how we engage the world.

Do you want to know the secret to confidence and security? Would it be nice to be happy and satisfied? Do you want to leave a legacy?

If so, commit—right now—to elevate your goal and vision for yourself and the world. The most powerful thing you can do as a human being and as a leader is to spend every ounce of your energy being present, aware, and connected to others.

That is how we engage.

What to Do When You Want to Disengage and Retreat from the World?

There is growing and powerful work that urges us to disconnect from our phones, stop responding to emails, and take time to reflect and think. Robin Sharma, leadership guru and global humanitarian, sees our isolation as a key aspect of our elevation.[4] This philosophy aligns beautifully with the LOVE system and the path to more conscious connections. It may seem like another confusing paradox, but conscious connections using the LOVE habit is actually a case for more space to listen, observe, and connect to values to elevate our consciousness and stay connected to ways we can make an impact in the world. The key questions are:

What are you disconnecting from?

What is your purpose?

Is your purpose to turn your talents, wisdom, and skills into works of art to elevate the condition of humanity? Is it to get in the best shape of your life and become a walking inspiration that shares stories about how you did it? Or are you running from anxiety and stress? Are you disconnecting to avoid LOVE?

> To experience the power of a conscious connection, you are not disconnecting or disengaging, you are shifting your LOVE. You are making deliberate choices about what to listen to, what to pay attention to, aligning your values, and engaging in deep reflection to elevate your life and the world.

That type of engagement isn't just good for the world. It's a balm for our hearts.

Conscious connections feel hardest when you find yourself immersed in a nightmare. There are things you do not want to hear. There are things that you do not want to see. You feel aligned with values, but also feel compelled to seek justice and fight against those that threaten your peace. When you're ignored, cut off in traffic, or diminished, you want to puff up, tap into your strength, and say, "That's enough" (like I did that day in the restaurant with my dad). Then one morning inevitably comes. You notice something strange. You are bone tired and weary. You have lost the strength and passion to fight. So, you do the only thing that makes sense, you disengage. Your emotions are blunted. You conclude that you just don't care that much about the world. And a new you emerges, void of light and passion. You have a new identity. Eventually, the disengagement and blunted experiences in life quickly turn into resentment and blame. Your search for relief is masked by more excuses to find a reason to retreat and disconnect. Your desire to villainize the world around you becomes an addiction. You Jones for it until, without warning, you have officially become a zombie.

How can we hold the power of conscious connections when things get really hard? It seems that disengaging is a pretty good option. When you practice listening to your inner guidance, listening to others without judgment and sharing the gift of your attention, you tap into your ability to make wise choices. As you sit quietly, it will be clear that you may need a nap or to say no to an event. You do this to protect your power so that you can be ready to LOVE. A conscious connection brings clarity about ways to find and have more joy. As you listen to your inner guidance, observe the world, examine your values, and speak with purpose and clarity, decisions will be clear. If your journey of self-discovery leads you to find a new job or transition to a new path, you will do so with joy, purpose, and passion. You will have practiced LOVE and made conscious connections that lead to a decision to expand, not disconnect. You are not leaving, you are growing. If LOVE leads you to a decision to end a relationship or get a divorce—throughout the journey, you can create a "shift" for yourself and listen to things that soothe your pain. You can observe the system of relationships and better understand the complexity of love and loss. You can make a commitment to stay aligned with your values, especially in the face of behaviors that feel hurtful or unfair. And you can engage by communicating your truth, finding a loving attorney or support system interested in well-being, and creating these pockets of bliss that turn something painful into possibilities. What you might see as a disconnection is really a new web of conscious connections that is pulling you to your purpose.

So, yes, we need to rest. Yes, we need quiet moments. Yes, we need to make hard decisions about people. Yes, we need to set boundaries to take good care of ourselves. But difficulty and pain are not excuses to take a day off from living. They are actually triggers to double down on your LOVE habits and to stay conscious about what matters most and connected to your power to impact your results.

Transform How You Lead: Wake-Up Call

I often hear from people who attend talks and realize how much conscious connection could improve their lives. While some get in touch with me quickly, most aren't as fast as Alesha. She'd attended a talk in Baltimore and booked a one-on-one session before the talk had even concluded. When she walked into my office, I understood why. She looked exhausted.

During our onboarding process, she'd told one of our legacy builders, the title given to all KUSI employees, about her stress. She'd taken a job out of college and risen through the company ranks, and everything had been fine—for a while. When her husband decided to quit his job and start a corporate tech security firm, she found herself taking on more and more responsibility for her work, her home, and their three teenage children.

"It's all too much," she told me. She paused, pressing her lips together in a tight line.

Sensing that she needed a listening ear, I nodded sympathetically, encouraging her to continue.

"I need help," she continued. "And I don't mean a housekeeper, personal assistant, or whatever." She looked down and sighed, shaking her head in disbelief. "I'm responsible for so many people. I feel like I'm drowning."

"What are your values, Alesha?" I asked, my voice gentle but firm.

She took a deep breath and set her jaw. Confidently, she answered, "Respect, love, and fun."

I sensed that she had more to say, so I jotted her values in my notebook, allowing her the space to share.

She continued, "I try to keep these values in mind—I know how important they are. I don't know if you remember me, but I was a volunteer for the shift. And, Talia, it was amazing. I need you to give me a shift *every day*." She laughed, the sound strained and humorless. Like a slowly deflating balloon, her confidence melted away. The strong, determined woman disappeared. In her place sat an exhausted shell of a person. "I just get too overwhelmed with everything."

I could almost see her amygdala firing.

When the fight-or-flight response is triggered, it causes our frontal cortex to shut down. The frontal lobe is the part of our brain responsible for goal setting. Back in the day, when there were "lions, tigers, and bears . . . oh my," our brains did not want us to reflect and think about how each creature might kill us. Taking the time to reflect would have gotten us eaten. No, we just needed to run. Today, we are no longer threatened by animals in the wild. We have jobs, policies, bosses, and coworkers that symbolize threats. And the same brain still shuts down with any perceived threat.

When you are emotionally triggered, you're not likely to connect immediately with your values and goals. I had to consider this when the CEO asked me to get his coffee. I knew my amygdala was firing. The LOVE system acronym can help keep your frontal cortex online. It is a task-oriented habit that will quiet the voices and soften your triggering responses to the world.

Your orders are to breathe and LOVE.

Although Alesha had all the tools to build a life around conscious connections, she still needed to actively *choose* that approach. She needed a decision point, something to make her actively choose LOVE. She needed a daily shift.

So, I pushed her. "You've mentioned my seminar, so I know you're familiar with the LOVE system. Have you tried conscious listening?"

"Yes!" she replied. "When I listened to myself, I realized that I was dwelling on my problems. I spent a lot of time fixating on the bad things in life: the boss I hate, how tired I feel, the family time I lost when my husband started his company. My son was telling me a story one evening, and I didn't even realize he was talking to me at first. I couldn't even hear him—my mind was too busy ranting about how I wished I'd responded to my boss earlier that day."

As she talked, I could hear her spiraling. I could see how this must play out in her life—because it was playing out right in front of me. So trapped in her own mind that she couldn't see how *she* was impacting those around her. Busy blaming everyone else for her problems, she hadn't stepped back to observe how *she* created dysfunction in all the systems of her life.

She needed a wake-up call. Having worked with thousands of people like Alesha, I recognized her problem immediately. She wasn't making the *conscious* choice to follow the LOVE system every day—it wasn't yet a habit for her. And it wouldn't be until she realized the misalignment between her current behavior and her values. That was the culture shot she needed. So I didn't even ask her about her observations—that would have to come later. Instead, I reminded her of how we'd begun the conversation. "Okay, let's focus on your values," I said. "Respect, love, and fun. Do you truly want to live those values?"

"Yes! Of course!"

"Then every morning—before you do anything else—I want you to customize an inner guidance script or a shift. And read it every day. Let me give you a sample to get you started."

She opened her notebook and looked at me expectantly.

"I am really enjoying the new ways I'm learning to respect myself and others. I really like the way that I'm showing up during this difficult time in my life. I respect how I face my stress and show up with love. I love my husband, so I'm delighted he is doing something that fulfills him. And when he's busy in the evening, I'm glad I get the opportunity to do fun things with my children."

She scribbled in her notebook for a moment. When she looked up, she quickly brushed a tear from her cheek.

"Can you do that?" I asked.

She nodded.

"After you do that, observe how your morning goes. Take a few notes about your interactions with others. For every good experience, do something positive for someone else. Get out of your own head and find something else to dwell on . . . like service."

Months later, Alesha enrolled in one of KUSI's small-group leadership trainings. She looked rested and happy. I was impressed by the way she engaged the group. No longer frazzled and apologetic, she brought a calming presence to the group. She carefully considered others' ideas, and when she shared her own experiences, there wasn't a trace of negative self-talk.

The real reward came after the class.

"Talia, I can't thank you enough for your help," she said, her smile bright. "I finally get it—you can't just be conscious on the days you feel good."

"That's great," I replied. I could see in her eyes that she finally got it.

We can't just practice conscious connections on our best days—because our best days only come when we choose to be conscious. It's when we're busiest that we need LOVE the most.

"And I have to share," she said, almost giggling. "Do you remember how I hated my boss so much?"

I nodded. "I do."

"Well, it turned out that he was going through a lot of stuff. His wife was sick. I guess I was making everything about me. You told me to do something nice for someone every day. I ended up doing several nice things for my boss."

"And what happened?" I asked.

"You won't believe it," she said, eyes wide. "He just retired. At the party, he thanked me for being so kind to him through his wife's illness. And get this—he chose me to replace him! I thought he didn't respect me—but when *I* started showing *him* respect, I realized that I was making a lot of assumptions that were not even real."

"That's awesome! And how's your family?"

"My husband's business is *booming*," she said. "It was hard at first, but once I realized what an opportunity it was for him, I couldn't help but be more supportive. Who wouldn't want to see the love of their life fulfill his dreams?!"

I remembered including a sentence about her husband in the assignment I'd given her—she decided to read aloud in the mirror. "Do you still read your inner guidance statements aloud every morning?" I asked, already knowing the answer.

"Oh, I don't have to read them anymore," she laughed. "I have them memorized."

"I'm so glad to hear that."

"Talia," she said, her voice suddenly serious. "I came to this training partly because I wanted to polish my skills for my new role. I also wanted to tell you something. That shift you gave me . . . it not only changed my life. I think it *saved* my life."

I nodded compassionately.

"Before I started practicing conscious connections, I didn't know what to do. I felt myself going into a dark place. Practicing LOVE helped pull me out. It saved my marriage, my job—even my relationship with my kids. I just wanted to thank you."

"You're very welcome," I said. "But the best way to thank me is to tell others. So we can change the world. Together."

Accept Your Power to Lead

To engage is to lead well. Let's create a shared idea of what it means to lead well. Leadership has long been the subject of scholarly research and debate, however, its definition remains elusive.[5] The Harvard Business School Centennial Colloquium has sought to address this by releasing their *Handbook of Leadership Theory and Practice*, an invaluable resource with over 800 pages offering valuable insights into various disciplines related to leadership theory and practice. Developing an understanding of what it means to lead sharpens our abilities as agents of change, allowing us to inspire collective responsibility and ultimately make positive changes in our organizations and the world.

What makes leadership so special is its ability to guide people toward achieving their goals in order to make an impact on society. By mastering leadership as a craft, we can make informed decisions that are based upon values and prioritize our actions accordingly. When done correctly, it can bring about innovative solutions that benefit everyone.

So, to foster better leaders and shape our organizations into something greater, we must develop a shared understanding of what it means to lead effectively. If communities around the globe act as value-based change agents, imagine the breakthroughs that could be made from millions echoing messages of love, kindness, and joy throughout society? Imagine the dreams we could weave together.

We are all leaders in our own right. We may not be fully aware of our power, but we are leading—and others are watching. In some cases, this gives rise to self-consciousness. We strain under the weight of expectations and judgments. But leadership—pure power—is about knowing, being, and doing. It's about being an example of a well-lived life.

We fantasize about influencing those around us to accomplish a mission or embrace an ideal. Many of us want to create a positive legacy but struggle to find the right approach. Unsure of how to bring others into our worlds, we cycle through the same tactics, continually disappointed by weak results. We search for the perfect mix of emotions and actions—that perfect cocktail that will help them realize "the dream."

How can we maximize our potential and create something meaningful? The answer to this question does not require a NASA supercomputer, but it does demand the same perseverance and attentive thought. Be and see the power you possess to influence change. From that place, learn to see others, and the world, as works of art that you will nurture and cultivate until *they* see *their own* value and power. I hope you see your potential to be one of the greatest leaders of our time. I hope you understand that you are leading others, even if you don't see it yet. I hope you can imagine yourself on a loving journey that ends in a purposeful destination. You can rise above the limitations of your current circumstances, improve your impact on the world, and create a legacy that lives on forever.

Wherever you are in your journey, I hope that the thought of leading makes you sit up straighter and listen harder. I hope you'll *own* the title of leader and realize that you are more than worthy of it. If you're ready to add more value to our world, if you want to join millions of people concerned about the future, then say, "That's enough!" It's time to embrace LOVE, become the power, and revolutionize the human spirit. It's time to engage.

TAKEAWAYS

In this chapter, we've discussed being consciously present in our lives by improving how we engage and connect.

We must first truly listen, observe, and live our values—then we can engage with skill. Learning to engage means taking responsibility for your actions. Engaging means mastering skills that support us in making effective choices based on conscious listening, keen observation, and clarity around our values. Like listening, learning how to engage and communicate with passion, grit, and grace will be the greatest investment that you will ever make in life.

The leadership skill enhanced by engagement is effective communication. The part of life most impacted by engagement is personal success and healthy relationships.

Below are key ideas to take with you:

- **Utilize the magic of reframing.** Instead of constantly complaining about the same issues, we should reframe how we approach a situation. Ask people about their values and find different ways to ask this question often. How do you interact with others? Are your behaviors aligned with your values? Are you conscious of others' values and value?

- **Remember the rules of engagement.** There are three simple, easy-to-remember rules: (1) Don't open your mouth without a purpose. (2) Preselect three core ideas that support your goals. (3) Plan to follow up and evaluate your results. Don't forget to respect others' time and get to the point.

- **Be present, aware, and responsive.** Remember the power of observation. Be aware of your surroundings and observe the mannerisms of the people around you to assess how to handle any situation and engage effectively.
- **Ask the right questions.** Success does not lie in having the right answers but in asking the right questions. Raise thought-provoking questions. Be more authentic, feel more connected, and achieve worthy goals.

- **Look inward.** Be consciously aware of the way you approach difficult situations. Acknowledge your own feelings of frustration or anxiety, but don't allow these feelings to control how you engage with others.
- **Live your values.** Consider the values you hold dear. Does shouting or forcing someone to do something align with values like respect and freedom? If not, consider adjusting your approach. Ask your family what they think. How can you collaborate and connect with ease?
- **Use the Fast 15.** My family's strategy can be a useful tool! Set a 15-minute timer and commit to actively engaging with one another until the timer is up.
- **Don't just practice LOVE on your good days.** The LOVE system is a daily practice. You must be committed to showing up for life, not just when you feel good. In fact, it can help you overcome your bad days.
- **Remember your values.** Remind yourself every morning of your core values and ensure that your actions promote those values.
- **Look outward.** We occasionally get so caught up in our own lives that we forget that other people struggle too.

- **Choose to practice the LOVE system habits during difficult times to make wise decisions about when to leave a situation or end a relationship.** Conscious connection brings clarity about ways to find and have more joy.
  - Listen to your inner guidance.
  - Observe the world.
  - Examine your values.
  - Speak with purpose and clarity.

And decisions will be clear.

*To know what is truly valuable, look
at what endures when all else fades away.*

—AFRICAN PROVERB

CHAPTER SIX

THE FINAL ACT: REVOLUTIONIZE THE HUMAN SPIRIT

———

From Depleted to Dancing!

People often convince themselves that they're hiding their pain. However, as a practitioner of the LOVE (listen, observe, value, engage) system who has taught thousands of classes on leadership, I can always spot the look of complete defeat. Sergio was depleted. Whether from crying or restless sleep, his eyes were puffy. His face seemed drawn, almost gray. And despite his best efforts, he couldn't hide his struggle. I learned later that he was the caretaker of two children with special needs. He'd recently lost a parent. And his wife was dealing with a chronic illness with a grim prognosis.

Despite his challenges, he showed up for a senior leadership program for an entire year. He took deep breaths, asked questions, and did his best to keep his eyes open. Struggling to stay awake, he sometimes politely stood in the back of the room during his fellow classmates' presentations.

He participated fully, fumbling through the learning process of what it means to step up to lead. Yet he was very graceful with his boundaries, choosing to pass when he had nothing left to give.

To date, Sergio has inspired me most. Regardless of his daunting list of challenges—all out of his control—he kept showing up for life. As we approached the leadership program's six-month mark, I noticed something very different about Sergio. He started to look alive—well-rested, hopeful, even energized. Curious, I asked him what had shifted.

He told me that he'd come to class two months earlier, ready to drop out of the program. Since he planned to tell me after class, he felt compelled to participate in the lesson that day. He saw an opportunity to receive one last lesson before he left the program. That day, we did a 90-minute session on the LOVE system to help improve work-life balance. We went through a series of exercises to increase skills and habits that support listening, observing, values, and engaging. After lunch, I asked for volunteers who wanted to experience the shift. Sergio was in the seat.

I began, as I always do, by asking him to tell me his values.

Sergio replied, "Family, integrity, nature."

"Great," I replied. "What is your biggest challenge these days?"

"I have so many challenges. I think I have bad luck. I feel like everything that can go wrong in life does. I'm not sure what it's all for. I feel tired all the time and sometimes spend hours dreaming about the fun I had in college. My job is a bit boring most of the time, and it seems like I never have time to hang with friends."

"That sounds tough," I told him. "I hope things get better for you." I paused, then made eye contact with him. Since I'd been listening to and observing him for months, I knew he could push himself beyond that framework. I asked, "Can you tell me another version of your life?"

"What do you mean?"

"Well, there are three versions to every story. One side is lined up with how you feel in the moment. Another side is lined up with how you want to feel in the future. Then there is the truth. The truth is typically irrelevant because we usually tell a version of our stories from a place outside of the 'storm.' In other words, everything you just shared is not technically happening right now in this moment. You are literally sitting in a chair in front of about 35 people talking about your life."

Perplexed, Sergio looked at me and cocked his head to the side. "Okay," he said. I could almost see the gears turning behind his eyes.

"Another way to pose this question is: Tell me how you're living your values."

"Well, I still might be confused, but I'll try."

He took a deep breath and exhaled slowly. As he did, I noticed his back straighten slightly against the back of his chair, his shoulders falling back naturally. *"I really like my house. I was so excited to surprise my wife and kids with a new puppy last year. His name is Rocco. We all love him. My children are so funny. I enjoy hanging with them. And my wife—she's had her health challenges, but I'm inspired by her strength. I really love spending time with her. I love going on camping trips with my family. It feels peaceful. I went fishing with one of my oldest friends last month. Best time ever."*

I replied, "Wow! Sounds amazing. Looks like you have a lot of wonderful things happening in your world. And what about your job?"

"You're not going to get me to like my job," he said. He laughed good-naturedly, and several others in the class joined in. All around us, the room's energy had shifted, as though a burden was being lifted not only from Sergio but from all of us. *"I do like my team's sense of humor, and I have a nice boss. She's so kind. The team got together and gave me a basket with my favorite foods when I had to be out for a week to take care of my wife. Oh, and this is weird . . . but for some reason, my administrative assistant, Betty—yes, I know it's cliche, but her name is actually Betty—makes the best cookies and pies. It makes me so happy."*

"If we had time, I would let you continue for as long as you could talk about this version of the story."

Again, Sergio looked up at me, bemused. After a brief pause, he went on. "Aren't you going to give me a shift?"

"You already gave it to yourself. Which is even better."

"How do you know?"

"Well, how do you feel?"

"Better!"

I told him, "That's the only thing we need today. So, tell me. What comes next?"

His face brightened, and he laughed a short chuckle that completed his transformation. "I want to feel like this more often," he said.

"Sergio! Congratulations, you just mastered this lesson. You get the point."

Five years later, Sergio enrolled in a one-day leadership workshop. I barely recognized him when he approached me at the beginning of class. He'd lost weight and his hair was noticeably shinier. I said, "Sergio! WOW! You look happy. How are things?"

He said, "Well, I'm so grateful. My wife is stronger than ever. The kids are good, and I feel great." He paused for a moment and grinned, his expression mischievous. "And . . . wait for it . . . I love my job."

I laughed along with him. As he talked, I was surprised that I remembered his story so vividly. "That's amazing," I said. "It's great to see you. What changed?"

"Over the last five years, I have committed to shifting; I do it every morning. I am not sure if I expected something to change. I decided to do it because it gave me so much relief."

"What an observation! Thoughts create feelings, and feelings inspire actions. Actions determine results. It is all connected."

Sergio said, "I took this class to find the answer to a question I've had on my mind lately. What happens when things are good? Can we stop the LOVE system? And does that mean I don't need the shift anymore?"

"Well, how about we try it? When I ask for volunteers, come up to see what the shift looks like when you're on top of the world."

After lunch, the shifting sessions started. Sergio was the fourth participant. The previous three people had been dealing with everything from divorce to losing a pet to being passed over for a promotion.

As I invited him to the front of the room, I once again marveled at the change I saw in him. I remembered the hunched-over, zombie-like man who I had met years earlier. Looking at him now, I couldn't help but look forward to watching him transform even further—to see just how good things could get for him.

"Welcome, Sergio!" I began "Tell me your values."

"Fun, freedom, patience."*

"Tell me about your greatest challenge these days."

"I used to call things challenges, but now I call them opportunities to have fun. Honestly, I'm just so darn happy."

"Tell us why you think that is. Do you have a secret?"

Tears welling in his eyes, he looked down at the floor, then back up at me. "I'm just so grateful!" he said.

"Instead of a shift, let's milk this gratitude." I stood behind him, taking my typical position for the shift, as he looked straight ahead. When we were both ready, I continued. *"Wow! I'm so grateful for life, friends, family, and fun. I remember a time when life felt hard, and I love the way I showed up through those times. I'm going to take some time brainstorming about things that make me smile. I'm going to take a walk and contemplate my biggest dreams and desires. I'm so excited about today and looking forward to tomorrow. I'm going to make a list of people I can help. Maybe I'll send out inspirational text messages to those I love. I'll dance the salsa with my wife tonight and celebrate the fact that she can move and dance. I'll laugh with my children. I'll tell people I love how awesome they are. I'll send my boss a thank you note for her kindness. I might pick up a pack of funny stress balls to share with my team. I'll eat something yummy. I'll watch the sunset tonight. I'll take deep breaths and share my story, strengths, and hopes."*

When I finished the shift, the room was quiet for a moment, and as I walked around to face Sergio, I could see that he was beaming. "Wow! Now, I have a bigger problem," he said.

---

* It is not uncommon for values to change to match up with how we are experiencing life. Some people share values that express needs or desires, while others share stable values that represent the things in life they want to prioritize.

"Please, tell me."

"I don't just feel happy. I feel like dancing and doing something that can help somebody. I feel like I can change the world."

"You, once again, have mastered today's lesson on conscious connections."

Power Requires Shared Energy

There's a reason I usually give shifts on stage, and that reason is directly related to my purpose. I'm not on that stage for myself. I'm not there for my family or even my company. The reason I stand on those stages is to spread LOVE.

In an auditorium, the room's combined energy acts as a sponge to absorb some of the change occurring on stage. The positive energy of one person's shift spreads throughout the entire crowd, buoying everyone in attendance.

We all experience a transformative shift, which embodies what many of us visualize as success. It manifests as a state of joy and satisfaction with who we are and what we're accomplishing in life.

One of my favorite definitions of success comes from Indian American bestselling author in the alternative medicine field, Deepak Chopra. Breaking through the pesky details to get to the core of how we all want to feel, Chopra suggests that success is about happiness.[1] It's about choosing goals we can be proud of and steadily moving toward those goals with ease.

We all want to expand, grow, be happy, and feel like we've used our limited time on this earth to do something purposeful. Everyone, no matter how rich or poor, or healthy or sick, has a yearning for *more* and *better*. Some are content with baby steps that move them forward in tiny increments. Like the wealthy children who throw themselves into charitable foundations, they want to make something better. They want to feel worthy of the space they take up in the room.

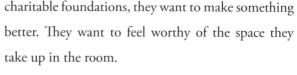

We all want to expand, grow, be happy, and feel like we've used our limited time on this earth to do something purposeful.

For others, that yearning requires a giant leap of faith—a huge push forward on a scale so grand that the people around them question their sanity. That was certainly the case for the little girl born in Mississippi to a mother who cleaned houses for a living. Although she never doubted her own potential, she couldn't have imagined becoming the billionaire she is today. Oprah persevered, consistently showing up and betting on herself day after day until everyone in America—and many people around the world—knew her name.

The human spirit is naturally *wired for progress*.

What about the millions of people who work hard every day? What about the people who seem to do everything right—if only they could catch a break? What about the men and women who end up

The human spirit is naturally *wired for progress.*

in prison, simply because they were in the wrong place at the wrong time? Or the employee who waits years for a promotion, only to see their boss retire or their company restructure, leaving them demoted?

How do we make sense of this world, where our results seem so varied and unpredictable? If the social system is to blame, what are the outliers doing differently? If success is built on charisma and good looks, how do we explain those who carve out their niche with neither? What is it that allows some to achieve their goals so easily? Some say it's simply hard work. Tell that to the millions of people who show up to perform backbreaking labor, day after day, for a wage that keeps their family below the poverty line.

Maybe some people just get lucky. I also think there's something to be said about the power of positive energy and encouraging thoughts. As thousands of self-help books argue, we can force the physical world to bend to our every desire—simply by harnessing the power of our minds. No matter what you believe, positive energy is powerful. There is power in numbers to achieve. It is simply easier to move a heavy object with the strength of many.

The LOVE system is designed to inspire and empower, and just like every system, it requires energy.

The LOVE system is designed to inspire and empower, and just like every system, it requires energy. It also produces energy. And through consistent engagement with conscious connections, we can all produce enough energy to light up the entire world. How do we leverage the power of conscious connection to transform how we live and lead in a world that feels so disconnected? As it turns out, there's a hack for that. I call it the LOVE system.

This book has described four changes that can bring you unbelievable results. I've seen lives turn around, money issues vanish, work problems disappear, and outrageous dreams materialize with this system.

And, while there are no guarantees in this world, if you show up as a leader—if you build your life around conscious connections—you'll see success. These are not grand claims. Open any book on leadership, psychology, habits, or success, or read the biographies of the most powerful leaders of our time. You will find that the takeaway will lead you down one of four paths. You will need to listen, observe, align values, and engage (or take decisive action). Research high-performing teams and you will discover that psychological safety (people feeling like they can make mistakes without feeling bad) bubbles to surface as the thing that has the biggest impact on results. Explore spiritual writings and principles of success. You will grow, expand, and find that the path brings you back to conscious connection through love. Your journey may not look the way you think it should, at least not at first.

That's okay.

The point is to start small, implementing these habits day after day. And before you know it, right in front of you, you'll see things begin to shift.

Tend to Your Roots

The little boy squatted, knees squeezed tightly into his chest and face buried in his hands as the hot Indian sun glowered down at him. All around him, his grandfather's crops slumped, brown and dry and rotten, insects searching their sagging leaves for the last traces of nutrients.

Vijay had failed.

Left alone while his grandfather embarked on a long trip, the child had been tasked with keeping the crops alive. He'd lost both parents at a young age. As a result, he craved approval, love, and belonging. His grandfather was strict, and Vijay often struggled to figure out what he wanted. And yet Vijay tried as hard as he could to please him.

When his grandfather announced his trip, asking Vijay to tend to the crops, the little boy felt a buzz of excitement. *Finally,* he thought, *this is my shot!* That first morning, he sprung out of bed, eager to go above and beyond to fulfill his responsibility. With onerous precision, he moved through the rows of plants, watering each individual leaf and each small, promising bud. He cared deeply about the plants. He visited each of them every morning and every night, taking notice of the curls of the buds and the ways the stems shifted in the breeze. Sometimes, he took a soft cloth into the field and gently wiped each leaf. He even spoke with the plants, encouraging them to grow big and tall.

A week had yet to pass before Vijay's casual talks with the plants grew more desperate—almost frantic. With each new morning, the plants looked sadder and sicklier. Once promising buds fell to the ground, and several stalks sagged. He'd driven a few stakes into the ground, giving the plants support as they grew toward the sky. Eventually, even the stakes weren't enough. Once tall and hearty, most of his grandfather's plants were now slumped, weak and brittle. So, the boy squatted there, sobbing, anticipating the sting of his grandfather's rejection, just one more disappointment in a life overflowing with them.

Almost without warning, Vijay felt another presence next to him. He wiped his eyes and looked up at his grandfather.

"I'm sorry," he begged. "I tried so hard to tend to your plants. The more I tried, the less anything worked. I'm so, so sorry. I failed, and—"

"Shh," his grandfather interjected. "Come here."

The boy stood, then lunged into his grandfather's arms.

Stroking Vijay's back, the old man explained, "You must take care of the roots and let the leaves tend to themselves. When you take care of the roots, you can let nature be."

Water Your Connections

As I reflect on Vijay's experience, I am immediately struck by the boy's hard work. After all, who among us hasn't had the experience of poring over a task, staring at a screen until our eyes are blurry and our backs ache, only to find that we've approached the task from the wrong angle? Hours of our work—tedious as wiping plants' individual leaves—were wasted. Not only did we feel like we failed. That failure cost us time and energy. When I read Vijay's story, I didn't see failure at all. I imagined a child who lost everything and is finally determined to start a new life. And he does so with care, compassion, and intention. He makes the wrong choice. But he makes it out of love.

The pain he feels as he watches the crops die likely began to exceed the fear of his grandfather's disappointment. After days of whispering encouraging words to every plant in the field, not only was he connected to his grandfather—but immersed in the world itself.

He made a connection with those plants. Even though he didn't know what to do, he listened, observed, and engaged. He showed up to the crops at three o'clock every morning, not out of obligation but because doing so aligned with his values. He'd committed to watching after those crops—he'd decided he would go above and beyond—and he did.

In the end, things didn't work out the way he'd hoped. He'd tried so hard to connect. And yet, because he didn't understand how the system worked, he ended up ruining the thing he cared about most.

So many of the people I meet share similar stories. People across the globe set their jaws, tense their shoulders, and tell me how determined they are to fix their workplace or heal their relationships. They have no idea what to do, but they decide to do it anyway.

When I see people like that—people who completely ignore the soil of their relationships—I teach them about listening, observing, valuing, and engaging. Most of us weren't born with these skills. Most of us are a lot like Vijay—we think we're caring for the people we love, but so often we're making superficial moves that care for the leaves and the buds. And we experience the pain of slowly watching our efforts and initiatives die in our hands.

When we finally realize that we should have been treating our challenges at the roots—listening, observing, valuing, and engaging—we understand why our efforts were so unreliable. We understand why we watched so many things we loved die.

Understand the system, care for the roots, and approach things with a reliable strategy. Spare yourself the pain of utter defeat.

That's the first lesson of conscious connections. No matter how lost, isolated, unappreciated, overwhelmed, or angry we feel—even when we're sitting in the middle of our beloved grandfather's dead crops—we can always move forward. And the answer is usually simpler than we think.

Water your connections. They are your roots.

Embracing the Power to Inspire

I have heard many versions of Vijay's story. One particular time, I was at a difficult point in my career. I'd begun to wonder whether leadership development was indeed a meaningful task. If we think about changing the world, we often imagine huge, intimidating actions—addressing world hunger, curing cancer, ending war. *How could I ever change the world? I'll never even come close to doing those things.* Instead, we plop down with our dead plants and sob into our hands until someone comes to save us.

When I think of Vijay, I often wonder whether anyone came to check on the boy. Did a single neighbor come by to see the child wiping the leaves or carefully pouring water onto the buds? Would they have told him what he was doing wrong? Would he have listened, or had he already decided he knew best? Would he have changed? Or would he have pressed forward, doing the same things he'd been doing, even when his approach wasn't working?

After almost 20 years of developing leaders, I had an idea. I was sitting on my deck, basking in gratitude as I looked up at the sky. Framing my view, the buds of emerging flowers peeked out from branches and vines. I reflected on Vijay's story and realized that *I* could be the neighbor who helped. *I* could visit the little boy and gently guide him to find a better way. *I* could listen to the fears and anxieties born from the trauma of his loss. *I* could help him see that he was loved. Then, maybe, we could get to work tending those poor plants' bone-dry soil.

This book—and my company, KUSI Global—sprung from that impulse. The skills in this book are the roots. Once you follow the system, habits will emerge, and the rest of your life will flourish. And when you feel that pure energy that comes from conscious connections, you'll want to tell others.

Some people are unaware of their power to inspire monumental change. Others seem oblivious to the harm and emotional scars they leave in their wake. We might all grieve if we knew the impact of our frowns, disengagement, and contempt. And our hearts would soar if we knew the impact of our words, actions, smiles, acts of kindness, and LOVE on the lives of others. That, more than any career accomplishment, is our legacy. If we want to show up every day as a leader, we must become conscious of our impact. We must connect with those we serve every single day. That's what it means to nurture conscious connections.

LOVE: Stay Conscious and Connected

Habits formed in childhood, whether good or bad, become precious possessions that you keep for life. So teach your children well that love is the key to true success, for it will open many doors and grant them a future of joy and growth.

—MAYA ANGELOU

Do you remember your first love? How your heart fluttered every time that crush came into the room? How your entire body engaged when you spoke with them, almost like your heart was threatening to beat out of your chest? What if you could feel that every day? If you have never felt love, I promise it's not too late. Practice the habits packed in the acronym LOVE, and you will. Except you'll skip right past the awkward teenage fumbles and get right to the meat of true love. I know because I do it every single day. I wake up in the morning and commit to authentic engagement. By listening and observing, I ensure that I'm conscious in this busy, disconnected world. Then I center my values and ask others about theirs. Finally, I commit to being present, aware, and connected to the world around me.

I have dedicated my life to developing skills that give me a greater capacity to live more connected to my evolving understanding of what matters. As a nonprofit leader, I knew that conscious connections were enough to save children impacted by HIV/AIDS. As a leadership development CEO, I realized that inspiring people could improve systems and achieve more meaningful results. As a single mom of two boys, I realized that love—patiently applied—could guide them through difficult moments in life. My deep sense of attachment and connection was enough to build healthy and productive relationships. Those seemingly simple acts are powerful.

And they demand real skills.

Pure power is watching yourself become a walking solution to a host of big and small issues. You walk into the room and your energy begins to heal, motivate, or encourage others.

Pure power is watching yourself become a walking solution to a host of big and small issues. You walk into the room and your energy begins to heal, motivate, or encourage others. I'll bet you have met someone that has done this for you. This pure power requires the ability to focus. If you can commit to focusing your heart, your intentions, your values, and your mission—if you can discipline your tongue to align your words with your purpose—you can communicate, stand, walk, see, taste, and hear as a reflection of your whole, authentic, true self.

The most common magic trick asks us to "pick a card, any card." So, which card will you pick? Will you continue to walk among the zombies? Or will you choose to engage?

Once upon a time, in the kingdom of music, there lived an orchestra of joy and harmony. Each instrument was unique and special in its own way. From the melodic strings to the thunderous drums, they all had their part to play. But something was missing—something that would give each performance depth and soul. That's when the fifth movement stepped into the spotlight—and what a remarkable piece of music it was!

The fifth movement was created with elements from all the other instruments, weaving them together with subtlety and grace. All of life's experiences were represented—from joys to sorrows, successes to failures, triumphs to defeats. Nothing was too small or insignificant for this symphony.

As each instrument played its part at just the right moment, something magical began to take shape. A soundscape emerged that filled listeners with awe and wonder, a beautiful balance between sadness and joy, challenge and solace. The audience was deeply moved by this unexpected masterpiece, feeling both inspired and comforted by its complexity and simplicity at the same time.

Your experiences and connections are like the fifth movement in an orchestra: they play beautifully together at the right moment to turn your life into one of wonder and awe for others to witness.

Listening, observing, valuing, and engaging are habits, skills, choices, and actions that create the magic. Essentially, they include everything that each of us has the power to master. You have complete creative freedom to decide how you use these habits to create meaning and rediscover your purpose. You will develop a craving to elevate the results you are striving for. The problems that we seek to solve might seem meaningless compared to a new way to live and lead. Striving to be both conscious and connected for the sake of happiness and joy will feel like a worthy outcome. The feeling that a conscious connection brings will be enough.

And, then, everything changes!

You're listening and gaining wisdom and peace of mind.

You feel more alive in the world and open to shared experiences.

You feel confident and decisive because you are clear about your values.

You are engaged and connected with others as you work together to work toward collective dreams.

You've unlocked the power of conscious connection! Now you can tap into your pure power and potential by mastering the habits of listening, observing, valuing, and engaging. You will bring clarity to your decisions, create meaningful connections, and transform the way you live and lead. Take this journey today and discover the joys of being both conscious and connected—where you will find the rhythm of your life awaits!

With these four simple habits, you can revolutionize the human spirit!

TAKEAWAYS

We've learned what happens when we accept the shift and reframe how we understand our lives. The LOVE system is designed to inspire and empower, and just like every system, it requires energy. It also produces energy. And through consistent engagement with conscious connections, we can all produce enough energy to light up the entire world.

How do we leverage the power of conscious connection to transform how we live and lead in a world that feels so disconnected? Show up daily for the four habits in the LOVE system.

Below are key ideas to take with you:

- **There are three versions of the truth.** The first is influenced by how you feel in the moment. The second is lined up with how you want to feel in the future, and the last is the often-irrelevant truth.

- **Always show up for your life.** No matter the circumstances, show up, care about yourself, and serve the people around you. Love and uplift yourself for doing so.

- **Practice the shift.** The shift is the art of reframing our perspective to get the energy we need to engage. Practice speaking about your life in terms of the things you love, things that make you happy, and things that promote your values rather than your misfortunes.

- **Tend to your roots.** Make sure that you are spending time on things that work and support an elevated goal.

- **Become a walking solution.** Use your power, time, and energy to heal, motivate, or encourage others.

- **Unlock the power of conscious connection.** Master the habits of listening, observing, valuing, and engaging.

APPENDIX

LOVE SYSTEM CHECKLIST

———

Master Conscious Connections with Self-Awareness, Reflection, and Intentional Communication

❶ Create new daily LOVE habits.

How well did you listen? Did you experience anxiety or serenity when connecting with others?

- What connections did you make today? Did you notice that smiling improved energy? Did you notice someone and ask if they needed something?

- What deliberate choices did you make to live your values? Did you give your family your full attention because you value them? Did you seek out an opportunity to see something breathtaking because you value beauty? Did you show respect to someone you dislike because *you* value respect?

- Did you ask questions, learn something new, and work on clear communication skills? Did you tell a story to inspire and uplift others?

❷ Create your own shift.

- What challenge(s) do you have? Share as you see it right now in this moment.
- What are your values?
- What words, ideas, and thoughts inspire you?
- What topics in your life excite you?

Craft a new story incorporating values and a new perspective that makes you feel energized. A good shift has a rhythm to it. You keep flowing statements that tell a new truth. Here are a few to get you started:

- This situation is not as it seems . . .
- I know I have the strength . . .
- I can feel a change happening . . .
- Although it feels hard now, as with all things, it is sorting itself out . . .
- Maybe I could achieve something amazing because of this . . .
- There are so many things that I really like about my world . . .
- I love . . .

❸ Evaluate your identity to check for limited beliefs and choices.

Part 1: Analyze yourself today as if you are a character on a show.

- As of today, I am the type of person who . . .
- What do you eat? How do you currently spend your days?
- What kind of job or work do you do?
- What kinds of people do you like or spend time with?
- What kind of attitude do you have? Optimistic or pessimistic?
- What habits fit your current personality?
- Can you predict the future of the character you are today as if you are watching your life play out in a movie?

Part 2: Find someone that inspires you. (Elevate the goal: pick someone [a muse] that you consider to be a world-changer or epic leader.)

- They are the type of person who . . .
- What do you think they eat? How do they currently spend their days?
- What kind of job or work do they do?
- What kinds of people do they like or spend time with?
- What kind of attitude do they have? Optimistic or pessimistic?
- What habits fit their current personality?
- Why do you admire them?

Part 3: Choose your identity. Look at the habits that your muse has. What choices can you make today to break limiting beliefs about yourself? What aspects of your identity no longer serve you well?

❹ Make conscious connections in work or business.

Reserve 15 minutes before or after meetings to answer several of these questions:

- Who needs to be heard?
- What parts of our business today will have the biggest impact on fulfilling our mission?
- Are our systems, choices, policies, and priorities aligned with our values? What are our values? Does everyone have a shared idea of what these values look like? Does everyone have a shared mental model of what these values do not look like?
- What do we want to be more conscious about? Is there a person on our team or a group that is being overlooked?
- What connections do we need to make between our choices and our business results?

❺ Identify three goals that you have for yourself, your team, or your business.

- If you doubled the impact of that goal or vision, what would the new goal be?
- Now, top that. What would be an even better goal to reach for?
- If there were absolutely no limits, what would be the ultimate goal?
- Now, top that. Try to keep elevating your goal until you cannot imagine anything greater. See how far you can go.
- Reflect: How can LOVE help me elevate my goal?
  - Just listen for answers.
  - Pay attention to cues.

– Contemplate your values.

– Engage with others. Ask others to help you with this exercise.

– See how they can help you top your biggest goals. Create new collective goals.

⑥ Invest in training around the following topics.

Create a rhythm of engaging in at least two meaningful learning activities (e.g., courses, books, mastermind groups, etc.) each year for the next five years.

- Emotional intelligence
- Systems thinking
- Cultural competence
- Communication
- Personal power

⑦ Be completely present in the world and stay connected to your power.

How do you do that? Listen, observe, value, and engage to access the portal to wisdom and miracles. Use a super-simple daily LOVE tracker:

Please rate the following statements based on your experience today, using the scale from 1 to 5 as described below.

1. Strongly Disagree

2. Disagree

3. Neutral

4. Agree

5. Strongly Agree

Respond to each statement by circling the number that best represents your experience. Please be honest and consider your experiences today only.

LOVE Assessment Statements

1. I noticed my listening choices today.

   1 | 2 | 3 | 4 | 5

2. I frequently stopped to observe the system of my life.

   1 | 2 | 3 | 4 | 5

3. The choices I made today aligned with my values.

   1 | 2 | 3 | 4 | 5

4. I communicated clearly and engaged others with purpose.

   1 | 2 | 3 | 4 | 5

Scoring

4–8: You may need to work on your awareness and engagement. Consider strategies for improving your listening, observing, and communication skills.

9–12: You are somewhat aware and engaged, but there is room for growth. Reflect on specific areas where you can improve.

13–16: You are generally aware and engaged in your daily life, showing alignment between your choices and actions.

17–20: Excellent! You are highly aware, and your actions are consistently aligned with your intentions. You are effectively communicating and engaging with others.

⑧ Elevate leaders and transform businesses.

Looking for guidance on becoming a better leader? Unsure of how to transform your business into a success? KUSI Global Inc. can help.

With a mission to improve the condition of humanity one skill at a time, we offer innovative leadership development programs and consulting services.

Visit our website at **www.kusitraining.com** to learn more about how we can help elevate your goals to transform how you live and lead. Together we can be more conscious and connected to create a ripple of impact in our world.

ENDNOTES

INTRODUCTION

1 Obama, Barack. "Remarks by the President at National Prayer Breakfast." The White House Office of the Press Secretary, 5 February 2015. Accessed 22 May 2023. https://obamawhitehouse.archives.gov/the-press-office/2015/02/05/remarks-president-national-prayer-breakfast#:~:text=I%20believe%20that%20the%20starting,in%20possession%20of%20the%20truth.

CHAPTER ONE

1 Harari, Yuval Noah. *Homo Deus: A Brief History of Tomorrow.* New York: Harper, 2017.

CHAPTER TWO

1 Tullett, Alexa M., and Michael Inzlicht. "The Voice of Self-Control: Blocking the Inner Voice Increases Impulsive Responding." *Acta Psychologica* 135, no. 2 (October 2010): 252–256. Accessed 22 May 2023. https://www.sciencedirect.com/science/article/pii/S0001691810001368.

2 Ibid.

3 "In Quotes: Apple's Steve Jobs." BBC.com, 6 October 2011. Accessed 22 May 2023. https://www.bbc.com/news/world-us-canada-15195448.

4 Lloyd, Joda, Frank W. Bond, and Paul E. Flaxman. "Work-Related Self-Efficacy As a Moderator of the Impact of a Worksite Stress Management Training Intervention: Intrinsic Work Motivation As a High-

er Order Condition of Effect." *Journal of Occupational Health Psychology 22,* no. 1 (2017): 115–127. Accessed 22 May 2023. https://psycnet.apa.org/record/2016-17141-001?doi=1; Jonsdottir, Inga Jona, and Kari Kristinsson. "Supervisors' Active-Empathetic Listening as an Important Antecedent of Work Engagement." *International Journal of Environmental Research and Public Health* 17, no. 21 (November 2020). Accessed 30 May 2023. https://www.ncbi.nlm.nih.gov/pmc/articles/PMC7662981/.

5 Kuhn, Rebekka, Thomas N. Bradbury, Fridtjof W. Nussbeck, and Guy Bodenmann. "The Power of Listening: Lending an Ear to the Partner during Dyadic Coping Conversations." *Journal of Family Psychology* 32, no. 6 (2018): 762–772. Accessed 30 May 2023. https://psycnet.apa.org/record/2018-25390-001?doi=1.

6 Schwab, Klaus. *The Fourth Industrial Revolution.* New York: Crown Business, 2016.

CHAPTER THREE

1 Cuddy, Amy J. C., Matthew Kohut, and John Neffinger. "Connect, Then Lead." *Harvard Business Review,* July–August 2013. Accessed 22 May 2023. https://hbr.org/2013/07/connect-then-lead; De-Coninck, James B. "The Effects of Leader-Member Exchange and Organizational Identification on Performance and Turnover Among Salespeople." *Journal of Personal Selling and Sales Management* 31, no. 1 (December 2011): 21–34. Accessed 22 May 2023. https://www.researchgate.net/publication/211384844_The_Effects_of_Leader-Member_Exchange_and_Organizational_Identification_on_Performance_and_Turnover_Among_Salespeople.

CHAPTER FOUR

1 Earley, P. Christopher, and Elaine Mosakowski. "Cultural Intelligence." *Harvard Business Review,* October 2004. Accessed 22 May 2023. https://hbr.org/2004/10/cultural-intelligence.

2 Faries, Mark D. "Why We Don't 'Just Do It.'" *American Journal of Lifestyle Medicine* 10, no. 5 (September–October 2016): 322–329. Accessed 30 May 2023. https://www.ncbi.nlm.nih.gov/pmc/articles/PMC6125069/.

3 Looney, Adam, and Nicholas Turner. "Work and Opportunity Before and After Incarceration." The Brookings Institution, March 2018. Accessed 22 May 2023. https://www.brookings.edu/wp-content/uploads/2018/03/es_20180314_looneyincarceration_final.pdf.

4 O'Bryan, Christopher J., Alexander R. Braczkowski, Hawthorne L. Beyer, Neil H. Carter, James E. M. Watson, and Eve McDonald-Madden. "The Contribution of Predators and Scavengers to Human Well-Being." *Nature Ecology & Evolution* 2 (2018): 229–236. Accessed 30 May 2023. https://www.nature.com/articles/s41559-017-0421-2.

CHAPTER FIVE

1 "Anxiety Disorders—Facts and Statistics." Anxiety and Depression Association of America, 28 October 2022. Accessed 22 May 2023. https://adaa.org/understanding-anxiety/facts-statistics.

2 Corey, Gerald. *Theory and Practice of Group Counselling*, 6th edition. Boston: Cengage Learning, 2019.

3 Bruhn, John G., and Stewart Wolf. "The Roseto Story: An Anatomy of Health." *Science, Technology, and Human Values* 5, no. 4, October 1980. Accessed 22 May 2023. https://journals.sagepub.com/doi/abs/10.1177/016224398000500408.

4 Sharma, Robin. *The 5AM Club: Own Your Morning. Elevate Your Life.* United States: HarperCollins Canada, 2018.

5 Nohria, Nitin, and Rakesh Khurana. *Handbook of Leadership Theory and Practice.* Cambridge, MA: Harvard Business Press, 2010.

CHAPTER SIX

1 Chopra, Deepak. *The Seven Spiritual Laws of Success.* San Rafael, CA: Amber-Allen Publishing, 2010.